Birds of the Chesapeake Bay

John W. Taylor

Birds of the Chesapeake Bay

Paintings by John W. Taylor

with Natural Histories and Journal Notes by the Artist

The Johns Hopkins University Press · Baltimore and London

To Marilyn, whose belief in me has made this book a reality

A Robert G. Merrick Edition

This book has been brought to publication with the generous assistance
of the Chesapeake Bay Trust and the Baltimore Gas and Electric Company.

Second printing, 1993

The Johns Hopkins University Press
2715 North Charles Street
Baltimore, Maryland 21218-4319
The Johns Hopkins Press Ltd., London

Printed in Japan on acid-free paper.

Library of Congress Cataloging-in-Publication Data
Taylor, John W. (John William), 1931–
    Birds of the Chesapeake Bay : paintings by John W. Taylor
with natural histories and journal notes by the artist.
        p.   cm.
    ISBN 0-8018-4380-4
    1. Birds—Chesapeake Bay (Md. and Va.) 2. Ornithological
illustration—Chesapeake Bay (Md. and Va.) 3. Birds in art.
I. Title.
QL683.C48T39   1992
598.29755'18'0222—dc20   91-45135

A catalog record for this book is available from the British Library.

Contents

Foreword

On cold winter mornings I love to hear the cries of the geese as they fly overhead. Their beauty and grace are accentuated by the brisk air and the light of dawn that casts vibrant colors on Maryland's great outdoors. When I hear the geese, the Chesapeake Bay comes to mind.

It is appropriate and timely that birds of the Bay are the subject of this book. In 1977 there were only twenty-seven active bald eagle nests in Maryland. By 1990 that number had grown to 115 pairs that produced 164 young. We have also been able to help other wildlife populations, including ospreys and great blue herons. In all this, the public is developing a new appreciation of the delicate balance between nature and the environment, as well as of the Bay as an ecosystem that is gaining worldwide attention.

The health of the Bay is vital, not only for waterfowl and fish and shellfish but also for jobs, recreation, and economic considerations. In Maryland we are working hard to insure that the Bay continues to thrive and be productive. Governor William Donald Schaefer is a leader who sincerely believes in the importance of the Chesapeake Bay and who has taken a major role in its recovery. And, of course, we have the support of the people—millions of them—who have taken active roles in helping the Bay and who are doing things that protect the environment.

This book, *Birds of the Chesapeake Bay,* is for everyone who cares. The wildlife it features is an important part of what makes the Bay special. In the fast-paced world of the nineties, it is easy to overlook the treasures of our wildlife resources. Artists such as John Taylor make us stop and look at what we have. John is a longtime friend of Maryland's natural resources. In fact, the Maryland Department of Natural Resources has enjoyed a long and productive relationship with him.

In 1959, John worked for the Maryland Department of Game and Inland Fish, the forerunner of the present-day Department of Natural Resources, as editor of the state's magazine, the *Maryland Conservationist*. He wrote and illustrated the stories, rendered artwork for the covers, and painted countless wildlife and natural resource subjects for state publications.

John provided the state with a painting of mallards for Maryland's first migratory waterfowl stamp in 1974. In 1979, he won a statewide competition for the stamp with his painting of wood ducks. In addition, his work is featured on four of Maryland's five wildlife conservation stamps and prints.

Birds of the Chesapeake Bay is a rare treat, then, from someone who really knows and loves our Bay and its natural resources. It combines art with educational information and narrative in journal form. John Taylor's journal entries conjure up vivid images and allow the reader to see the wildlife, the habitat, and their interaction through the eyes of the artist.

I am sure that you will enjoy this wonderful book, and I hope it will inspire you to work to see that the birds of the Chesapeake Bay are enjoyed by future generations.

Torrey C. Brown, M.D.
Secretary
Maryland Department of Natural Resources

Preface

It was back in grade school that I first felt the fascination for birds that was soon to become an avocation and eventually the driving force behind my choice of art as a profession. The spark had been kindled by a fourth-grade teacher who had formed an Audubon Junior Club and then, seeing my interest, encouraged me with special attention.

I was soon spending much of my free time chasing after birds, tramping the woods and fields with a tiny opera glass (which I recall had a 3x magnification). These after-school excursions, always within walking distance of home, led to all-day trips to destinations attainable by public transportation. A few years later, I began to participate in field trips conducted by the local Audubon Society to more distant locations. It was on one of these forays that I enjoyed my first view of the Chesapeake Bay.

Although I was only sixteen at the time, I wrote a long account of that day's observations, of the great flocks of wildfowl settling on the Susquehanna flats, the colors of the sunset sky, and of the marshes that lined the shores of the Bay. I wrote of an immense raft of canvasbacks, nearly a mile long, on the Sassafras River. I described the hundreds of swans flying across the horizon, brilliantly backlit by the lowering sun.

That account was one of the earliest entries in a journal that I kept of my field trips. At first these were hardly more than lists of the day's birds, but they were expanded, with more details, when I was intrigued with a new bird or an unusual behavior pattern. Places of exceptional interest also inspired more elaboration. During my last year of high school, I kept a carefully written journal, illustrated with pen and ink sketches, of birding trips.

There followed, however, a long hiatus when other matters prevented me from keeping any written account of the few times I could spend afield.

In 1963, shortly after moving to Mayo, Maryland, near the shores of the Chesapeake, I resumed the journals, recording not only trips afield but also observations closer to home. These notes, which now fill four loose-leaf binders, I have continued to this day. It is from these writings, largely from 1971 on, that the selections in this book have been excerpted.

My first bird book, which I used as a field guide, was a slim, pocket-sized volume by Chester Reed, illustrated with paintings. It was the study of these pictures that first introduced me to the artistic representation of birds. I remember especially the artist's attempt to capture the deep reflective blues of the indigo bunting, which change with every angle of light.

My own clumsy attempts at drawing birds in those grade-school days (again at the instigation of this dedicated teacher) were meager efforts at imitating the paintings in the guide. It was not until much later, after I had already been out of school a couple of years, that I began to take art seriously, to consider it as a profession.

The inspiration came while I was employed by the Division of Birds at the Smithsonian Institution in Washington, D.C. There I met several artists who were then working on the mural-like backgrounds of dioramas, and I had the opportunity to watch them at work. I saw them transform an empty space into an open field, a shadowed forest, or a quiet marsh. I think it was then that the idea to follow art as a profession took root.

Once I felt the sense of satisfaction and release given by creative work, no other field of employment offered any appeal. Indeed, I was quite miserable doing anything else.

To many, including relatives and close friends, the idea of earning a living by painting birds was a preposterous folly, a hopeless dream. They counseled me against it. One friend compared my obsession with that of Captain Ahab's for the white whale. It would destroy me, he predicted. But because I did not want to be miserable, I persisted.

It was just at this time that I was called into military service. Rather than let this interruption distract me completely, I used the opportunity to visit bird artists in England and in Germany, where I was eventually stationed. I searched them out and visited them in their studios. These contacts served to strengthen my resolve to develop whatever artistic ability I might have.

After discharge, I returned briefly to the Smithsonian, then enrolled in art school. This decision finally gave me the opportunity to spend much of my time painting, always with birds as the primary subject matter (much to the annoyance of my teachers). I continued to keep in close association with established bird artists—at least with those who responded favorably to my letters—and visited with them.

After art school, I spent a few years as artist-editor for the *Maryland Conservationist* magazine, published by the Department of Game and Inland Fish (now the Department of Natural Resources). But the need to devote more time to painting led me to embark on a full-time free-lance career.

Since that day as a youth, seeing the Chesapeake for the first time, to the days when I came to work in Annapolis, and now while living at Pennington Pond, near Mayo, Maryland, I have found special inspiration in the Bay. Its creeks and marshes, and its bird life, particularly the migratory waterfowl, continue to be an endless source of joy and stimulation. Also inspiring to an artist has been that pale opalescent quality of light that illumines Chesapeake waters and tints the loblolly pines and tawny marshes of the lower Delmarva Peninsula.

For nearly thirty years, I have sought out this beauty, plodding through the marshes, walking the beaches, and journeying by canoe up the myriad streams that wend their way to the Bay. Rare was the day when I did not manage to spend some time afield, if only on a late afternoon hike. I have, with camera, sketchbook, and notebook, attempted to record the excitement and richness of these experiences. And I have built up a store of memories that I have called on in each of the paintings in this book.

It is my hope that a bit of the beauty of the Chesapeake, with its unique blend of water, land, and marsh, and of the wild creatures that live there, will be reflected in the pages of this book.

Birds of the Chesapeake Bay

March 20, Pennington Pond

Just passing through are two blue-winged teal, a mated pair, that dabble briefly at the edge of the lapping tide. They find some sustenance, possibly animal life, in the sediment along the shore, which looks barren and lifeless. Certainly no vegetation, submerged or emergent, grows there.

They spook wildly, almost frantically, while I believe I am still at a safe distance. Blue-winged teal are usually a trusting species, but this pair may have been under great hunting pressure on its wintering territory.

April 6, Sellman Creek, Anne Arundel County

The cattail marsh in spring displays a delightful tawny umber, washed with tints of yellow-green. A few spikes are still fluffy with seed and some stems still stand, straight and tall, despite the buffeting by a winter's wind and storms. But most of the plants are broken and fallen, many broken off cleanly, as if by the snip of scissors. The floor of the marsh is carpeted with these fragments.

Busily feeding among this vegetative debris is a pair of blue-wings, each swinging its head from side to side, as if sifting the water through the bill. More teal join them, a mixed batch of blue-wings and green-wings. Something upsets one hen blue-wing; she quacks continually, quite like a mallard.

April 21, Deal Island Wildlife Management Area, Somerset County

The spacious marshes here are home to the very few blue-wings that nest in the Chesapeake system, so I hoped to find a nest or spot a brood of ducklings. I find I am too early in the season.

A few pairs are already mated, but most blue-wings are still in the courting phase. In threes and fours, they course over the marsh in pursuit, though there is not always a hen in the lead. Possibly there are territorial motives behind the chase, or a pair resenting the intrusion of an unmated individual. At times the pursuit seems more playful than in earnest.

Definitely serious are three drake blue-wings that dart over the reeds, following a hen that then settles in a stretch of open water. The drakes immediately surround her, bobbing their heads and giving the peeping call. A moment or two later, they are all off again.

My approach startles one pair, loafing atop a grassy tump. The drake, alerted, raises his head and calls in alarm, the same peeping plaint. He slides into the water and paddles away, his mate remaining in place.

September 12, Bristol Landing, Patuxent River, Anne Arundel County (by canoe)

Wild rice has been heavy with seed the past few weeks, and the birds have been gorging on it. The red-winged blackbirds discovered it first, then the bobolinks arrived, and the sora rails came through. Now the blue-wings have come to feast on what is left.

Many rice stalks have fallen into the spatterdock, spilling seed into the water, where the teal can find it. Ducks jump ahead of me at every bend in the river, flashing their chalky blue wing patches. Once in flight, they course over the marsh at great speed before settling back to feed.

Family groups of wood ducks flush, shrieking, with the teal, and there are a few mallards and even a pair of gadwalls. It looks as if they are also feeding on the fleshy, globular fruits of arrow arum, which swirls about in the currents and washes up on the shoreline. Several kinds of smartweed are also ripe for harvest.

Despite widespread loss of habitat, the blue-winged teal (Anas discors) remains among the most numerous of North American waterfowl. According to recent surveys, it ranks third in total numbers, behind the mallard and northern pintail. It is appreciated by the hunter, who finds it an elusive target and a tasty addition to the game bag, and by the naturalist, who values it because of its beauty and the life it gives to the marshes.

Perhaps the adaptability of the blue-winged teal is the key to its success, to the relative stability of its numbers. Although its primary nesting territory is the pothole country of the northwestern prairies, it also breeds along the Atlantic Coast and in Texas and Louisiana. The Chesapeake nesting population is not significant and is centered on the lower Delmarva Peninsula.

When there is heavy rainfall and streams flood the lowlands and create new wetlands, more blue-winged teal stay south to nest. During times of drought, they readily move to another area, not so affected. Few species of waterfowl are as flexible.

The drake blue-winged teal is recognizable by its small size, the white crescent in front of its bill, and the light blue patches on the forewing. The brownish, mottled hen also has the light blue wing mark.

JOHN W. TAYLOR

February 5, Pennington Pond

A pair of wild black ducks has joined the half-tame mallards for the free meals here. The drake is as fearless as the mallards, some of which feed from my hands. However, his mate has never lost her fear and retreats to a safe distance.

Today a very high tide makes it difficult for the ducks to reach the scattered corn once it settles to the bottom. Because the grain is too deep for them to reach by their usual dabbling or tipping procedure, the mallards resort to diving several feet beneath the surface (supposedly the "puddle" or river ducks are unable to dive).

The drake black duck dives with them, so buoyant that he immediately returns to the surface. He submerges with the same forward plunge of a canvasback or other diving duck.

I have seen tame mallards dive after corn, under these artificial conditions. Now there is proof that black ducks will also dive. Would they do so under more natural circumstances?

April 14, Piney Creek, Queen Anne's County

With loud quacking, a black duck burst from a tangle of briars and poison ivy in the loblolly woods near the landing. A brief search revealed her nest, on the ground and obscured by the heavy undergrowth.

Nine creamy eggs were carefully cushioned in a pocket of pine needles, mixed with bits of brownish down that the hen had plucked from her own breast. With the down were a few dusky flank feathers.

When I returned to the landing later, I purposely stayed clear of the site so as not to disturb the bird any more.

December 4, Camp Letts, Sellman Creek Trail, Anne Arundel County

Feeding in the wide "lagoon" portion of the creek was a variety of waterfowl, though not in large numbers. Eight hooded mergansers, diving vigorously, kept close together, while scattered about were a few buffleheads, canvasbacks, and a single goldeneye. A dozen black ducks swam near the shore.

Among the black ducks were two whose olive-colored bills and lighter coloration showed them to be youngsters, born this past summer. These two, jerking and bobbing their heads rapidly, followed and nudged another black duck. One uttered an odd, growling quack.

This seemed a courtship behavior, quite unexpected this early in the season, and especially unusual because it involved immature birds. Most waterfowl courtship activity occurs in late winter or spring.

However, a bit of research later showed this to be quite normal behavior for black ducks. Biologist Vernon Stotts, who carefully studied the species on the Chesapeake, wrote that "immature females begin pairing in December, when they are only six months of age." Adults form sexual attachments in September, even though breeding does not begin until March and April.

Alone among North American native wildfowl, the black duck (Anas rubripes) is confined to the east. Although it breeds in scattered numbers across the northern tier of states east of the Mississippi, the center of its abundance is along the Atlantic Coast. It nests along both shores of the Chesapeake Bay, but in higher numbers in the salt marshes of the Eastern Shore.

Although the black duck closely resembles the hen mallard in size and body conformation, it is much darker in coloration. In good light, the contrast between the light head and darker body is noticeable. The somber-hued hen mallard shows little color difference between the head and body.

In flight, the flashing white underwings of the black duck are more conspicuous than those of the mallard. Close and in good light, the dark bluish purple speculum in the wing of the black duck is distinctive. It is not margined with white, as is the mallard's paler blue speculum.

Black ducks are present the year round on the Chesapeake, but are more readily observable in fall and winter. Their numbers are then augmented by new arrivals coming from farther north to winter on the Bay. During breeding season, from March to July, they retire to more isolated habitats and stay close to cover.

Hunters find the black duck without equal as a game bird. Intelligent and wary, it has a spirit of untamed wildness that earns the respect of all who come to know it.

January 12, Kent Island, Queen Anne's County

A cold front has brought brisk winds and a clear sky, the horizon glowing bright red after the sun sets. Against this crimson backdrop, flocks of waterfowl are on the move, thousands of them dropping into a cornfield. Many are pintails, flying with more grace and precision than the mallards and geese with them. Tight groups of pintails sweep over the field, twisting and turning in unison, dark against the sky. Others of their kind drop out of sight, below the tree line. The constant clamor of Canada geese adds to the confusion and excitement.

As it grows darker, another silhouette appears atop a cedar copse—a great horned owl, watching the scene with more than casual interest.

February 1, Pennington Pond

The half-tame mallards on the pond are great as decoys. Today they attracted a splendid drake pintail to the flock. First seen tipping in midpond, he did not fly wildly at my approach, as is usually the case with the wild ducks that come. Nor was he tame. He nervously swam off to a good distance.

(At first he showed no interest in the food I had given to the mallards, but he stayed around and gradually learned to feed with them. Eventually, he even came up onto the lawn to feed and became fairly tame.)

October 28, Hunting Creek, Alexandria, Virginia

The Hunting Creek estuary, entering the Potomac River just south of the Woodrow Wilson Bridge, is surely as polluted and filthy as it looks.

So I was quite surprised at the large number of waterfowl here today. At least one hundred ruddy ducks, two dozen shovelers, several hundred coots, scattered black ducks, and many mallards were present. Most surprising of all was a large mass of pintails milling about in the sky.

I first noticed the pintails as the whole company lifted out of a bed of hydrilla, growing so thickly that it appeared as an island or mud flat. The ducks circled about, several times settling as if to land, then flared off. Finally, they came to rest in a stretch of open water.

It was a spectacular performance, the snowy breasts of one hundred drakes flashing as the birds twisted and turned in the air.

Are these pintails newly arrived, following the cold winds just now blowing in from the north? Or have they been in the area for awhile, subsisting on the hydrilla?

The northern pintail (Anas acuta) inhabits the entire northern hemisphere and thus enjoys a wider distribution than any other species of waterfowl. In North America, northern pintails are more common in the West, and so the Chesapeake has never been prime territory for them, even in earlier times. Yet they winter in good numbers on the Delmarva Peninsula. Most of them breed in the far north, many beyond the Arctic Circle.

In flight, the pintail is trim and slender, with a longer neck than other puddle ducks. The long central tail feathers of the drake may extend one-fourth of his total length. The chocolate-brown head and the white strip up the neck of the drake are also identifying marks.

The hen pintail is a mottled brown, a lot like the mallard female, but the greenish brown speculum on the wing distinguishes her, as do her slim proportions.

John W. Taylor

January 12, Pennington Pond

The pond has been locked in ice for more than a month. No waterfowl have been seen, except on the open waters of the Bay, beyond Thomas Point. Now the thaw of the last few days has opened water along the shoreline, where tidal action has broken the ice. With the appearance of even the smallest patch of open water, the mallards are back.

Six of them were busy tipping and dabbling at dawn. They found something to eat under the water, though there is very little submerged vegetation here. Perhaps they discovered animal matter of some sort.

Later in the day more mallards returned. Some made awkward landings on the ice, sliding and slipping on the watery surface. Several dozed in the sunshine or preened while resting on the edge of the ice.

November 17, Pennington Pond

Early today the tide is quite low, but no wind or breeze stirs the water. The pond is unusually calm, glasslike in its smoothness. Close to the shore, near some downed phragmites, is a commonplace scene—simple and subdued, but of extraordinary beauty.

Ten mallards float above their reflections, in a variety of poses and angles. The effect is of gentle curves and soft roundness, heightened by the near-perfect reflections. And the whole is bathed in early morning light, warm and mellow.

One drake rouses himself, stretches a wing, then lays his head to rest again, restoring the tranquil rhythms of the composition.

November 26, Sellman Creek, Anne Arundel County

A dozen black ducks flush from the creek's upper reaches, uttering soft quacks of protest at being disturbed. The receding tide, an especially low one, has left but a thin rivulet meandering between muddy shores, and the ducks wade on the flats, feeding.

Like most black ducks, these are wily, wary birds. They spook at my approach, not like the much tamer mallards, which sometimes consort with them. This group consists only of blacks, pure-bred natives, keeping to themselves.

The mallards are farther downstream, where the creek widens. A tight flotilla swims, silhouetted against the fading light, trailing wakes that mar the dead-calm surface. Unlike the blacks, the mallards allow close approach before merely swimming to a safer distance.

So today the blacks and mallards, though closely related, do not intermingle at all. Yet the fear is real that the genetic purity of the native black duck will be lost through interbreeding with pen-raised mallards.

The glossy metallic green head of the mallard (Anas platyrhynchos) readily identifies the drake. Hens are light brown, with darker brown streaks and spotting. Both sexes, in all plumages, may be recognized by the violet-blue speculum (an iridescent patch on the inner wing) bordered with black and white. Only the hen gives the familiar quacking call; the note of the drake is a low whistle, seldom heard.

There is controversy over the mallards that live in the Bay area. Are they truly wild? Does the introduction of pen-raised birds somehow taint the genetic strain of the native stock? Should money be spent to provide more natural habitat rather than on artificial propagation? Regardless of one's stand on these issues, it must be admitted that mallards add life and interest to many locations where the native waterfowl population has been greatly reduced. Released birds may be found at marinas and boat landings, and they nest in gardens and backyards.

Although it is not always easy to separate them from captive-reared birds, there are truly wild mallards on the Chesapeake. Prior to the release program in the mid seventies, there was a relatively small wintering population. Banding recoveries indicated that these birds had nested in western Canada and in the prairie states.

February 7, Muddy Creek, off Rhode River, Anne Arundel County

The first of many parties of geese passed overhead, just before sunset, moving toward the creek's wide estuary. Honking all the while, the geese passed high over the water, turned back, and began to descend. Side-slipping to lose altitude, several geese turned briefly upside down as they dropped. They slid into the water, joining a dozen swans and a scattering of black ducks.

There was a constant din as other flocks arrived, some circling to reconnoiter, others coasting directly in. Passing flocks called with high-pitched urgency; birds on the water sounded more confident. In the growing darkness, geese continued to come, all from the east, where they had been feeding in cornfields. Each evening they seek the quiet security of these open waters, where hunting is not allowed.

The gathering must have totaled over two thousand birds, all in full voice. The sound was ear-splitting. None of them was aware of my presence until I moved to leave. Then suddenly the noise ceased completely, and the closest geese swam rapidly away. In the darkness, they must have heard the rustle of leaves, or caught some movement.

March 2, Popham Creek, off West River, Anne Arundel County

It was overcast much of the day, then low clouds darkened the horizon late in the afternoon and rain looked imminent. Spring peepers piped from the swampy pools at the head of the cove, and a single chorus frog chimed in with its strange, raspy trill. A lone chickadee whistled its spring song, but an eerie hush, a calm before the storm, remained.

Then, abruptly, the urgent, excited honking of Canada geese shattered the quiet. To the south, the sky was filled with wildfowl. Battalions of geese approached, breaking into tumultuous disarray when they reached West River.

Some planed down on set wings, as if to settle on the water; others regrouped, then kept on course to the northeast. A few turned back to the south. The clamor of at least five hundred geese rent the air. Contributing to the bedlam were about sixty-five swans, flying with the geese.

Though some birds obviously wanted to stop and rest, eventually all continued their journey, passing to the northeast. The racket faded as they disappeared. Five minutes later, the quiet returned; there was not a goose in sight.

March 26, Choptank River, Dorchester County

Borne on gusty winds from the south, snow began accumulating as I reached the Choptank River. A mild spring morning had suddenly become a cold, wintry afternoon. Within an hour, green pastures and blooming trees were whitened, and blowing flurries blurred the landscape. A grove of red maples, wine colored with spring flower, glowed through the smoky drifts.

Hundreds of Canada geese, feeding in wheat stubble, lifted into the ghostly mists, honking excitedly, then disappeared in the haze. Other flocks rose, half-hidden in the opaque atmosphere, then dropped back to earth. Nothing apparent was disturbing the geese, and I wondered if they were merely reacting to the storm.

I almost left the scene without noticing the bald eagle in the gray distance, perched ominously on a bare snag.

Many people are familiar with the Canada goose (Branta canadensis) and its resonant honking call and black head with the white chin patch. Hunting the Canada goose has become both a tradition and an industry on the Delmarva Peninsula. More than one-half of the Atlantic population of this species winters on Chesapeake waters.

But few people are aware that until the late fifties the Canada goose was not common on the Bay and was rarely hunted there. Prior to that period, the principal wintering grounds of the goose were farther south, mainly in North Carolina. The introduction of the mechanical corn-harvesting process, with the attendant waste left in the fields, was largely responsible for keeping the birds in Maryland and Delaware. The ready food supply, combined with the easy access to large bodies of water, provided ideal conditions.

Recent declines in the wintering goose population on the Bay may be due to intense hunting pressure and to additional food resources now available in the northern portion of their winter range. Each year more geese remain in Pennsylvania and New York, rather than move to heavily hunted regions farther south.

Also of recent occurrence is the tendency for more geese to become nonmigratory, year-round residents on the Chesapeake. Many are now breeding far south of their normal range, utilizing wildlife refuges, parks, and even golf courses.

The principal nesting range of the Atlantic population of the Canada goose lies far to the north, in the tundra zone of the Ungava Peninsula. Migratory flocks begin arriving on the Chesapeake by the third week of September, their numbers increasing through October. Most leave for the north in early March; some are gone by late February, and others linger into April.

February 7, South River, Anne Arundel County

All day yesterday it snowed, a dry, fluffy ten inches. At dawn today, the last of the storm is visible, a heavy layer of clouds just under the rising sun. South River is a wide, white expanse, with but a sliver of open water, reflecting the saffron-pink of the horizon.

On this ice-free pool float two dozen tundra swans, only partly visible above the heaped ice and snow. Their alabaster whiteness, blending with the bluish white of the snow, combines with the sky's pale pinks and yellows to create the most subtle of color harmonies. Five swans rest on the ice, their sinuous necks and bodies in twisted repose.

Later, in groups of threes and fours, they take to wing, crossing the river toward Thomas Point. Their trumpeting carries clearly from the far shore, a distance of at least two miles.

March 13, Pennington Pond

The past week has been exceptionally mild, with winds from the south. Such conditions at this time of year stimulate the migratory instinct of tundra swans, and indeed many of them have been on the move.

At quarter of eleven tonight, as the moon shone through fleecy clouds, I heard the clamor of swans, high up and far away. The sound was softened, mellowed by the distance as it gradually faded to the north. A half-hour later, I heard more swans, also quite high and flying in the same northerly direction.

Where would they put down? Pennsylvania? The Great Lakes?

After midnight, more swan music, much closer than that heard earlier, carried over the waters of the Bay. This most likely came from the local population, which is still with us.

November 18, Muddy Creek, off Rhode River, Anne Arundel County

The fading light threw a marsh-side pine into shaggy silhouette. Only the rustle of red-winged blackbirds, settling to roost in the phragmites, broke the chilled hush of winter twilight. Suddenly a low croak, followed by a series of loud hoots, punctuated the quiet. Above their reflections floated ten swans, calling, heads lifted to the sky.

A single resonant whoop from above announced the arrival of six more swans, planing in on set wings. After they splashed into the water, there was great commotion—guttural croaking and whooping, accompanied by much wing-flapping and head-bobbing. After this initial flurry of greeting, the flock continued to converse in low, throaty tones.

Then, abruptly, one swan lifted its head and gave forth a sustained trumpeting, neck extended, bill pointed skyward. The others accompanied this solo performance with husky, murmuring sounds.

Four more swans then glided in, huge wings cupped, set for landing. A pair already on the water greeted them with a duet of frenzied yelps.

By then all light had drained from the horizon, though reflections from the moon danced on the water. As day ended, the contented quacking of feeding black ducks drifted from the darkness across the creek.

Since early times the Chesapeake has been the most important wintering ground in all of North America for the tundra swan (Cygnus columbianus). During the early seventies, official surveys on the Bay counted an average of forty thousand swans. This totaled ten thousand more than their number in any other region.

However, since the deterioration of water quality in the Bay, and the subsequent loss of food plants, larger numbers of swans have moved on to North Carolina and Virginia. Recent surveys have shown that North Carolina can claim more than one-half of the Atlantic Coast population of tundra swans. The 1991 Chesapeake count totaled 23,100 swans.

Swans that winter in the Bay area have drastically altered their feeding habits. No longer able to find their traditional staple of submerged aquatic plants, they have resorted to gleaning waste grain left in the fields adjacent to tidal waters. They may travel ten to fifteen miles to find corn or soybeans or to graze upon shoots of winter wheat.

When the Bay was healthy, swans fed almost exclusively on wigeon grass and various species of pondweed, which grew in brackish estuarine waters.

Tundra swans nest far to the northwest, in Arctic regions beyond the tree line from Alaska east to Baffin Island. In autumn, their return trip to the Atlantic Coast involves flights of exceptionally long distance. They fly day and night, and rest stops are infrequent and widely spaced. The first swans arrive on the Chesapeake in mid October, but most do not arrive until a month later, especially if the weather is mild. They remain until about the third week of March.

John W. Taylor

November 5, Blackwater National Wildlife Refuge, Dorchester County

The roar of several thousand snow geese shatters the quiet of late afternoon as they explode from distant marshes. A low-flying helicopter has frightened them. The tumult created by such a mass exodus is deafening. The whirling swarm aimlessly mills about for a time before dropping back into the marshland. But the geese cannot settle down. Restless, they lift off again, fall into separate flocks, then cross to an adjacent cornfield. After a few moments, they again take flight. Each time they take off, their high-pitched yelping increases in volume and intensity.

Among the imposing gathering of snow geese is a substantial number of dark-phase birds, formerly known as "blue geese." Indeed, they outnumber the white birds four to one. Most of these blue-gray geese are richly colored adults, with a mottled, harlequinlike pattern on the head and body. Only a few younger birds, paler of hue, are among them.

The preponderance of blue-phase geese here is evidence that these are *lesser* snow geese, a race more common in the Midwest and West, nesting west of Hudson Bay.

November 6, Kent County

Overnight the wind had shifted to the northwest, and this morning it is still blowing with considerable force. Against this wind, in brilliant early sunlight, snow geese drop into a field surrounding a farm pond. The sun, still quite low, burnishes each bird with salmon pink. Immediately upon landing, every goose assumes a crouching position or rests upon its belly, in order to gain some respite from the wind. For a half-hour the flight continues. The geese arrive in groups, some of them hanging in the wind, almost stationary, before chuting to the earth.

All are in the white phase, immaculate against the deep blue sky, and with the brilliant light glowing through their wings.

November 25, Blackwater National Wildlife Refuge

Amid much noise and commotion, snow geese feed on the roots of cordgrass. Their thin, nasal voices carry a resonance and blend with those of the Canada geese foraging with them.

I hear the grunts of the snow geese as they pull at the rootstocks. Now and again, one snatches a bit of vegetation and runs away with it.

November 27, Church Creek, Dorchester County

I heard the loud chatter and babble of snow geese, but I could not see them, either in the sky or on the ground. Following the sound, I determined that it was coming from beyond a hedgerow, bordering a cornfield. Judging from the contented tone of their voices, I guessed that the geese were feeding.

As I started to move nearer, the whole flock rose in one clamoring mass. I assumed that they had only *heard* my approach, for I was still out of their line of sight.

Some flew toward the nearby Little Choptank River, but most circled back. They did not resettle and resume feeding, but continued to mill about restlessly.

I was wondering if my presence alone had put such a scare into them when a northern harrier appeared, skimming the fields. At times its course took it into the midst of the confused geese.

Two races of snow geese (Chen caerulescens) visit the shores of the Chesapeake. The bulk of those that winter on the Delmarva Peninsula are known as greater snow geese, an eastern population that nests close to the Arctic Circle on Baffin and Ellesmere islands. Snow geese of this race migrate exclusively along the Atlantic Coast, south to North Carolina.

The lesser snow goose, which winters primarily in the Midwest and West, includes among its numbers a substantial proportion of dark forms, especially east of the Great Plains. Known as "blue geese," these were formerly considered a separate species.

In recent years, snow geese have increased considerably on the Delmarva Peninsula. The increase can perhaps be attributed to a change in feeding habits rather than to a rise in numbers. At one time they fed almost exclusively on the rootstocks of coastal plants; recently, they have found the corn left behind by mechanical pickers and have flocked inland.

Greater snows are slightly larger than lessers, but are indistinguishable in the field. Both species are all white, with black wing tips. "Blue geese" have blue-gray wings and heads, and the body appears mottled.

March 15, Horsehead Farm, Queen Anne's County

Earlier it had been warm with clear skies, but at dusk the sun fell behind a curtain of fleecy, gray-blue clouds, lending a suffused, rosy flush to the horizon. These pastel tints, reflected, danced across the waters of Prospect Bay

Silhouetted against this fading light, three birds passed, flying at exceptional speed. The mellow, doubled whistle of the green-winged teal identified them. Two hens and a drake, they were probably engaged in mating or courtship display. They rapidly flew over a marshy promontory, fell beyond a grove of pines, then returned to complete a circle. One drake veered suddenly downward, twisting about with marvelous dexterity, then rose to rejoin the others. They raced in a wide circle across marsh and water, turning and tilting, dropping and rising.

April 23, Black Swamp Creek, Patuxent River, Prince George's County

I could hear the cricketlike call of green-winged teal, although I could not see them because of the very tall grasses growing on both sides of the creek. I made my way through this growth to the water's edge, where, well hidden, I watched eight of them busily feeding.

Obviously already mated, there were three pairs of green-wings and a pair of blue-wings. Their heads partially submerged, they sifted water and mud through their bills with a swinging sideways motion. I could not tell what they are finding to eat in the muck.

One richly colored drake suddenly became suspicious. He lifted his head and looked directly at me. However, he soon relaxed and resumed feeding, walking with a lively gait across a drier stretch of flat. Two more teal sailed in very close and were about to splash in when they saw me and awkwardly changed course in midair.

October 28, Dyke Marsh, Alexandria, Virginia

Despite the close proximity of a major highway, a hen green-wing swam calmly amid the cattails, not bothered by the din of heavy traffic. But she flew off when she sensed me watching her and joined a group of her kind around a bend in the stream.

Partially concealed amid the marshy growth were about forty teal, the drakes still in various stages of the "eclipse" plumage, or late summer molt. Most had nearly regained full winter dress, but all retained mottled henlike feathers on their flanks. Some squatted, resting on the tidal mud; others swam lazily about, dabbling in the water.

The late sun glinted on the metallic greens of the speculums when the birds paused to preen, and on the green eye patches of the drakes.

An inhabitant of marshes and narrow tidal streams, the green-winged teal (Anas crecca) is not often seen on the Bay's open waters. Rather, it sifts the muddy bottoms or wades the shallows in search of the seeds of aquatic plants such as smartweeds, sedges, and rushes. It likes to feed on the mud flats at low tide.

The Chesapeake is not a primary wintering area for the green-winged teal. In recent years, it has been estimated that about two thousand of them spend the colder months on the Bay. More are likely to be seen during the migration period, which is at its height in November and April.

Teal are the smallest of waterfowl, and often their size alone is enough to identify them. The green-wing is shorter of body than the blue-wing, with a stubbier neck. At a distance on the water, the vertical stripe in front of the wing is often the most conspicuous mark. Up close, the chocolate-brown head, with a green iridescent eye patch, is distinctive. The green speculum on the wing is seldom visible when the bird is swimming.

The closely related, very similar European teal is a rare visitor to Chesapeake shores. It lacks the vertical crescent on the side and instead has a longitudinal stripe on the scapulars.

John W. Taylor

April 23, Black Swamp Creek, Patuxent River, Prince George's County

Even from a distance, it was obvious that the heronry still prospered. A steady procession of great blues moved to and from the site, tucked under a bluff at a bend in the creek.

All of the nests were high in a tall grove of sycamores, still bare and gaunt against the fresh greens of spring. The largest tree, a towering giant, supported about fifty nests, and an adjacent sycamore, almost as large, held thirty-five or forty. Flimsy structures, made out of twigs and small branches, some of the nests looked imbalanced and insecure. They were of various sizes, suggesting that some may have been old ones, newly repaired.

The lanky forms of the herons, standing next to their nests, repeated the rhythms of the thin, pale tracery of the sycamore limbs. On nearly every nest was a sitting bird.

Other herons were busy with housekeeping chores. One landed, legs and neck dangling awkwardly, with yet another stick in its bill. Others rearranged their scraggly domiciles, pushing and shoving material already collected.

A faint but continuous murmur droned from the depths of the colony. Palpitations in the throats of the herons finally indicated the source of this eerie sound. There was an occasional croaking squawk, more like the call of a black-crowned night heron than the usual harsh cry of a great blue.

From my vantage point across the marsh, I watched the herons without disturbing them. The scene was one of connubial joy and contentment; each pair at a nest and, as yet, no hungry mouths to feed.

May 20, Island Creek, Queen Anne's County (by canoe)

Canoeing upstream along a wide brackish marsh, I reached the confluence of the main stream with a smaller tributary shown on the map as Granny Finley Branch. On one shore stretched an extensive cattail marsh; on the other rose a steep hillside topped with a grove of tall pines.

Peering down at me from these treetops, necks craned anxiously, were four or five great blue herons. As I paddled under the bluff, other herons came into view, perched on lower branches. Some stood next to bulky nests of sticks, flimsy flat platforms, which looked more substantial than most other heron nests I had seen.

Protruding from several nests were the scraggly, ragged heads of the young herons. The youngsters were clad mostly in natal down, a light grayish blue, and their heads were partly feathered. Three young near the edge of one nest were strong enough to stand upright. Four more nests were placed among dead branches of a giant beech tree nearby.

July 28, Pennington Pond

It takes nearly a half-hour to accomplish, but a great blue manages to swallow whole a full-sized crab. First the heron struggles with its captive, dropping it several times into the water, then hastily retrieves it. For ten minutes or so, it merely holds the crab, as if pondering the predicament. Then only the legs of the crab protrude. After a few moments the crab disappears down the throat of the great blue, grossly distending its gullet as it passes through to the crop. What powerful digestive juices this creature must have! And how tough are the walls of its alimentary system!

Widespread and common on the Bay and its tributaries, the great blue heron (Ardea herodias) is known colloquially as the crane. Almost every stream and farm pond has its resident heron, and numbers of them congregate where conditions are favorable, on larger bodies of water. Isolated nesting colonies, consisting of from ten to one hundred pairs, are found throughout the watershed, where there is suitable habitat and freedom from disturbance.

Reaching four feet in erect stance, the great blue is the largest heron. Basically bluish gray, there is white on the head, with tints of cinnamon on the neck and the leading edge of the wing. Three or four dark plumes extend from the back of the head.

The great blue does not attain its fully adult plumage until eighteen months or older, when it has reached breeding age. The young bird has a slate-colored crown, rather than a white one, with much cinnamon on the wing coverts. The neck lacks rufous streaking.

With neck drawn in and feet extended behind, the great blue flies with slow, deliberate wingbeats. When startled into flight, it utters a harsh croak, repeating the call several times if especially agitated.

A few great blues remain on the Bay even during the coldest winters. Returns from banded birds indicate that these are likely to be migrants from farther north. Local breeders move to the south, some as far as Cuba and the Bahamas.

April 13, Pennington Pond

This is a delicious spring morning, the air crystalline, sparkling in the early light. High on an oak's bare branches crouch three night herons, taking in the sun. Their outlook commands a view over the Bay, to the tree line of Thomas Point, and beyond, to the Eastern Shore. The whole scene is bathed in virginal light.

The three, grouped together, seem tired, completely relaxed, not at all alerted by my intrusion. I guess that they are just passing through, resting after a long flight the night before. Had they been present earlier I surely would have noticed them. I briefly admire their crisp, almost elegant black, white, and gray feathers before I leave, not wanting to disturb either their rest or the scene's tranquility.

September 5, Beverly Beach County Park, Anne Arundel County

The late summer gathering of night herons is increasing. Fallen branches along the shoreline shelter ten of them, both adults and the somber immature birds. Many others are scattered about in the upper branches of nearby trees. It is late in the day, and as it grows darker they stir about, several of them flying out to the Bay's open waters. They head in the direction of the fish traps set offshore, which by day are crowded with fish-eating birds—herons, gulls, and cormorants. Other night herons move across to the far shore of the pond, uttering their peculiar single squawk. In addition to the usual call, there is a higher pitched note, a sort of barking squeal. At first I thought there was a fox nearby, but I continue to hear this sound, its source moving as the herons move.

September 8, Beverly Beach County Park

For the past two weeks, night herons have gathered on the ponds, joining the many great blue herons and egrets that have been here much of the summer. Twelve black-crowneds were arrayed among the waterside trees and on downed branches over the water. The top of a Virginia pine partially concealed others.

At bank-side, I flushed a brownish immature night heron almost at my feet. Its startled "quok" alerted still other night herons in the trees above. Most of them crossed to the far shore, where they sought perches among the other herons. After much scuffling and squawking, they finally quieted, but remained restless, still regarding me with suspicion.

Later I saw three of them, dark chunky silhouettes, atop pilings in the Bay. Yet another stood motionless in the water, where the outgoing tide washed from the inlet.

Like many birds of the Chesapeake, the black-crowned night heron (Nycticorax nycticorax) has suffered considerable reduction in numbers. Once there were several nesting colonies near Baltimore and Annapolis. Now breeding seems restricted to the lower Bay and the Atlantic Coast, except for one colony near Baltimore. In most instances, night herons nest among groups that include several species of herons.

Away from these breeding stations, night herons are most often seen during spring and fall migrations or as part of a late summer dispersal. Night herons use the Bay as a flyway when moving north and south.

Short and stocky, the night heron does not have the gangling frame of most herons. The top of the head and the back are black with a greenish gloss; the breast is white, washed with gray on the sides. Several long white feathers form a plumelike crest on the back of the head. Immature night herons, grayish brown with light streaks, are more difficult to recognize.

May 28, Beverly Beach County Park, Anne Arundel County

I had long wished to find a nest of the green-backed heron and searched in vain many times in likely locations. Today my chance finally came when a green-backed flew from dense undergrowth carrying a whitish object in its bill. I could not tell whether it was eggshell or excrement, but in either case the bird had revealed its nest site.

A shallow tidal pool separated the hiking trail from the tangle of briars, vines, and shrubbery from which the bird flew. After working my way around the pond, being impaled by greenbriers, and extricating myself from the constrictorlike vines, I came upon the nest.

Situated head-high in the main fork of a black willow, the structure was about a foot and one-half across and made entirely of willow twigs. A foot long or more, the twigs averaged about one-quarter inch in diameter. Smaller ones lined the pocket, and a few larger ones were woven into the platform's base.

In the nest was an indeterminate mass of fluffy gray. I discerned the yellowish bills of two newly hatched herons and then discovered a third hidden beneath them. Too weak to lift their heads, they seemed exhausted. A scant coat of grayish down, though long and bushy about the head and belly, left much of the pinkish body exposed.

Neither parent showed itself while I was near the nest.

June 14, Beverly Beach County Park

Returning today to the nest, I discovered that the young herons had prospered and were perched side by side next to the nest. My noisy approach alerted them, and they instinctively froze. They stood with necks extended and bills pointed skyward, a stance much like the hiding posture of the bittern. Though the down still clung to the belly and head, they were clad mostly in pin feathers. The front of the neck was still quite bare, as were the throat and lores. Securely supported on thick yellow legs, the youngsters remained motionless, except for a slight swaying from side to side.

Not wanting to disturb them further, I stayed at some distance, hoping to see the parents bring food. Neither appeared during the twenty minutes I waited.

December 18, Pennington Pond

A green-backed heron, feeding late today at the pond's edge, is quite unexpected. Though twice before I have seen this species on the Bay in December, it usually leaves for the south in September. Never have I recorded a green-backed this late in the month.

The heron looks healthy and vigorous as it stalks fish on the incoming tide. The winter thus far has been mild, with no ice yet, possibly explaining the tardiness of this bird, which still shows the heavily streaked breast of an immature, born this past summer.

The harsh, explosive squawk of the green-backed heron (Butorides striatus) is often the first indication of its presence. Usually rendered phonetically as "skeow," this call is given not only in alarm but also in territorial disputes and in courtship rites. Were it not for its loud voice, this heron would be far less familiar than it is.

For, despite its healthy numbers and wide distribution, the green-backed is otherwise quite unobtrusive. It is a solitary fisher, waiting in quiet, patient ambush for long periods. At such times it hardly tolerates the approach of even its mate. And it is a master at skulking and hiding when it does not want attention.

It is especially secretive at nesting time. On the Chesapeake, it selects locations that are most inaccessible to people, then places its nest deep in the densest growth of briars and vines. It takes care not to be seen leaving or approaching the nest.

In other parts of its range, the green-backed may occasionally nest near others of its kind, though rarely in large colonies like other herons. Group nesting, usually of no more than six pairs, is most likely in the wilder, less settled portions of its range.

A warm-weather species, the green-backed does not appear in its Chesapeake haunts until spring is well advanced. Nearly all depart south by October.

John W. Taylor

January 9, Pennington Pond

Mallards on the pond apparently attracted an eagle. The eagle at first hovered over the ducks, then swooped low over the water on great cambered wings. The mallards quacked nervously but did not take flight. The eagle appeared to be trying to frighten them into flying or was perhaps searching for a weakened or injured individual.

It was an immature eagle, probably three or four years old, as evidenced by its nearly white head. Otherwise, its plumage was dark brown, with a few light feathers showing in the wing.

After the hovering flight, the eagle perched on a bare oak stub, at moderate height and directly above the mallards. For ten minutes it remained there, turning its noble head and massive bill. It was close enough that a leg band was visible.

Abruptly it took flight, once more dropping near the water, hovering and circling. Again the mallards did not fly, but resumed their anxious quacking. This time the young eagle came to rest at some distance, in the crown of a tulip poplar. For ten to fifteen minutes it remained motionless, before launching into the air and heading for the open waters of the Bay.

March 21, Sellman Creek, Anne Arundel County

Two bald eagles excitedly call at the head of the creek. One is a fine, full-plumaged adult, and the other is a brownish immature bird, with splotches of white on the body and wings. The white-headed adult, perched in a pine, is the more vocal, giving its shrill cackle repeatedly. The other, perhaps made nervous by my appearance, takes flight, then hesitates, circling, before alighting on the same pine.

At length, my presence seems too much for them, and they both take to wing. They fly in the direction of the nest at the head of nearby Glebe Creek.

April 22, West River, Anne Arundel County

The eagle nest here is well situated for observation. One can drive the dirt road to the nearby hillside and watch the nest at eye level. The adult eagles appear relaxed as long as I stay in the car; when I stand outside they seem nervous but do not leave.

The two eaglets are well feathered now and seem quite dark all over. All of the white natal down has disappeared, and they lift their heads well above the nest. One adult perches near the nest, quiet and motionless for much of the afternoon.

The other adult appears, soaring in lazy circles, at times quite high. The fish it is carrying glistens in the sun. Gradually it approaches the nest, but still seems to soar aimlessly. Why doesn't it come to feed the young?

I realize that my presence disturbs the circling eagle, although its mate still perches calmly near the nest. So I return to the car. Immediately the eagle drops to the nest and begins tearing apart the fish, feeding bits of it to the young. The eaglets eat slowly, swallowing the food rather than bolting and gulping it down in the usual manner.

After feeding the young, the eagle joins its mate, still perched sedately near the nest. They remain within a few feet of each other for about a half-hour, then both take to wing, cavorting playfully as they fly toward Rhode River.

With a wingspan of almost six feet, the bald eagle (Haliaeetus leucocephalus) vies with the great blue heron and the tundra swan as the largest bird on the Chesapeake. Bald eagles do not attain the white head and tail until the fourth or fifth year, the younger birds being dark overall with light splotches on the underwing, body, and tail.

The bald eagle's staple diet consists of dead or dying fish, supplemented with carrion. The bird occasionally captures live waterfowl, but these are almost always ill or crippled individuals; eagles cannot outfly healthy ducks or geese. The bald eagle also takes fish away from other predators, especially from the osprey.

The breeding cycle begins in midwinter, when the bald eagle begins collecting material for nest-building. In most cases, it renovates a nest used the previous year. The female lays two or three eggs as early as February, but it is often July before the young leave the nest.

The Chesapeake region is one of the bald eagle's last strongholds. Only Alaska and Florida can boast higher populations of nesting eagles. And their numbers are increasing, after a serious decline in the seventies, attributable to DDT poisoning and the destruction of nesting habitat.

April 1, Beverly Beach County Park, Anne Arundel County

A new osprey nest crowns a telephone pole near the beach. This nest is quite close to the structure used last year, also atop a telephone pole, which seems still in good shape. Surprisingly, the birds have moved even closer to the edge of a housing development.

The pair is on the nest, the female already incubating, though she returned only two weeks ago. The male launches into the air, screaming, and swings directly overhead, protesting my nearness, but returns to the nest within minutes. Tilting his head to watch me, he continues to call.

Another nest, also with a sitting osprey, is within sight, 150·yards up the beach. It adorns a platform over the water, erected expressly for ospreys. The nest seems much too close to the pair nesting on the telephone pole. I would not have thought they could tolerate each other at such close quarters.

Then I see two more ospreys, hanging in the breeze, fewer than 75 yards from the platform nest. Five birds are in sight at once! Is there a third nest so close? I see a partial one, a scattered pile of small branches at the end of the jetty.

Three nests within a few hundred yards! This almost forms a colony of nesting ospreys. I have heard of osprey colonies elsewhere, but I had thought this species was more territorial here on the Chesapeake.

April 3, South River, Anne Arundel County

The nuptial or courtship flight of the osprey is in full display these days. The male mounts high in the sky and, hovering in one place, screams with exuberance and high spirit. He may hang like this, as if suspended, for ten minutes or more, his call, softened by the distance, filling the spring sky. Finally, the bird plummets to earth, swooping to perch near his mate—the object of the whole performance. Often, the pair will then engage in swift mock pursuit, twisting and turning, dodging and veering, low over the water.

August 8, Pennington Pond

A bit after the first light of day, I heard ospreys shrieking angrily, highly agitated. The harsh cackle of an eagle followed. Upon investigating the ruckus, I saw an osprey repeatedly diving into the top of a tulip poplar. Focusing on the direction of these attacks, I could make out the white head of an eagle, its body hidden by foliage.

The osprey then left, flying out over the Bay, but returned almost immediately, screaming fiercely. Again it swooped at the eagle, throwing out its talons in its fury. Suddenly, another eagle appeared low over the pond, then rose to perch back in the woods. It remained only a few minutes, then both eagles took flight, disappearing beyond the tree line.

I have frequently observed ospreys highly agitated by an eagle's presence. Is it only because eagles often steal fish from them?

The osprey (Pandion haliaetus) is one of the very few birds found on every continent. Yet its distribution over this vast range is far from uniform. In most areas the osprey is uncommon, and in some parts it is quite rare. But in a few favored localities, such as the Bay, it is abundant.

Here, the osprey seems to find the necessary ecological conditions and freedom from human persecution. A ready supply of fish and a wide selection of nesting sites are available. The osprey utilizes duck blinds, tall trees, navigational buoys, piers, and telephone poles for nest platforms.

Ospreys arrive at their Chesapeake breeding ground in March (an Eastern Shore tradition maintains that they show up first on Saint Patrick's Day). Most of them depart for winter quarters before the end of September. Those seen later in fall are late migrants from farther north.

September 16, Otter Point Creek, Harford County

Over the wide expanse of marsh, two harriers hunt, tilting and swaying in the wind. Flaring suddenly, the first drops into the grass, displaying the wonderfully intricate barred patterns of its wings and tail. The facial pattern is quite dark, and the flanks are a rich russet, marks of the first-year plumage.

The young harrier rises with a catch that resembles a clump of vegetation in its talons. Possibly there is a rodent somewhere in the cluster.

October 25, Patuxent River, above Hills Bridge, Anne Arundel County (by canoe)

Showing rich, chestnut-tan underparts, an immature harrier careened over the shrubby marshlands. Twice it paused, hanging in the breeze, legs dangling, then dropped out of sight beyond the vegetation. Very soon it was aloft again, coursing along the river's edge.

At the same time, high overhead, a red-shouldered hawk traced circles in the sky. A fine, rose-chested adult, it dropped suddenly, wings folded, in a headlong dive. Veering upward just above the marsh, it swung to perch in a maple sapling.

The red-shoulder's presence seemed to intimidate the young harrier, which made dives and feinted attacks at the larger hawk. Then, yet another red-shoulder rose from the marsh, calling excitedly, a wild piercing scream. But they must have settled their differences amicably. In a few moments all three hawks were together, soaring lazily over the marsh.

October 28, Western Branch, Patuxent River, Prince George's County (by canoe)

Unseasonable warmth has caused heavy morning ground fog the past few days. Today there is an even thicker haze, lasting until nearly noon.

Out of the mist, a hawk appears, ghostly, and comes to rest atop a stake driven into the marsh. As I drift closer, I see a female harrier, seemingly unconcerned by my closeness. She fluffs her plumage, lifts one foot to her bill, and seems quite relaxed. She finally takes flight when I slide the canoe onto a grassy tussock, trying to steady it so that I can take a photograph.

December 14, Centerville, Queen Anne's County

While scanning the waterfowl rafted on the Chester River, I was surprised to see a harrier swoop over them and then, legs extended, drop to the surface of the water. The ducks, mostly scaups and canvasbacks, took no evasive action, neither diving nor taking flight. The harrier flew a short distance farther, then hovered once more close to the water. It attracted the attention of a few herring gulls, one of which veered sharply toward the raptor.

The northern harrier (Circus cyaneus) belongs to a cosmopolitan group of raptors, of medium size, long of wing and tail. Birds of open country, they hunt by patrolling close to the ground in search of small mammals, birds, and reptiles.

Harriers show decided sexual differences in coloration. The adult male is predominantly grayish blue on its upper parts, with a brownish cast. The head and chest are the same color, while the belly is lighter, almost white and spotted with cinnamon brown. The female is a much darker grayish brown, heavily streaked with darker brown. Immature harriers look a lot like the female, but generally show more rusty red. In both sexes, the distinctive white rump is the best field mark.

The Bay lies near the southern extremity of the harrier's breeding range. Thus most birds seen in these latitudes are either migrants or wintering individuals, though recent surveys have discovered definite evidence of nesting.

About twenty pairs are thought to nest on Maryland's Eastern Shore. The core breeding area is along Fishing Bay and the lower Nanticoke River in Dorchester County and near the Deal Island Wildlife Management Area in Somerset County.

John W. Taylor

March 10, Pennington Pond

Two hawks perched together atop a pond-side sweet gum remain motionless for a half-hour or so. One is a richly colored, full-plumaged adult, with much rusty color on the upper wing coverts and the intricately barred breast. The other is a somber, brownish immature, with streaked rather than barred underparts.

The older bird takes flight first, flapping then soaring over the woods to the north. The other follows directly after it. Both are, rather untypically, silent.

I had seen these birds together several times and assumed the younger to be offspring of the other. Now, however, they are acting like a mated pair, and at this season no bird born last year would still be consorting so closely with a parent.

April 8, Pennington Pond

The crows raised a louder ruckus than usual this morning. Clinging to thin branches atop an oak tree was the object of their anger—a great horned owl. Joining the fracas was a pair of red-shouldered hawks!

Along with the crows, the hawks made diving passes at the owl. Their wild screams punctuated the steady din of cawing. The hawks flew alongside the crows, pursuing the harassed owl each time it took flight.

This wild scene presented quite a turnabout. The crows frequently had mobbed this same oddly matched pair of hawks (one is in immature plumage), but today the crows ignored them. The owl was a more formidable enemy.

April 10, Muddy Creek, off Rhode River, Anne Arundel County (by canoe)

At midmorning, very high in a deep cerulean sky, a pair of courting red-shouldered hawks soared, screaming continuously. Their shrill, excited cries carried clearly, even from such great heights. Several times, as they passed close together, the higher bird dangled its feet loosely.

Suddenly both half-folded their wings and began a long, slanting descent to earth. The higher bird, the smaller male, followed closely, its cry vibrating with intensity and vigor. Both extended their legs, hanging limply beneath them, the whole time.

A few moments later I noticed that one of the pair had returned and, dropping low, carefully scanned the ground below it, as if hunting. Then it abruptly changed direction and moved off toward yet another red-shoulder, approaching in the distance. I saw all three soar over the tree line, until they disappeared.

May 20, South River Farms, Anne Arundel County

I have suspected that red-shouldered hawks nest in these woods, which crown the ridge between Selby Bay and South River. Often I have watched them in the sky here, soaring alone or in mating flight. So when I saw one carrying a sprig of fresh green leaves (used to decorate the nest), I carefully marked its line of flight.

I found the hawk perched on the rim of the nest, situated in the main fork of a willow oak, about twenty-five feet high. Surprisingly tame and docile, it merely turned its head to look down at me. I had expected some protest at my intrusion.

The red-shouldered hawk (Buteo lineatus) is perhaps the most frequently seen of the hawks that live in the Bay area. It has adjusted better than some species to the loss of the natural woodlands that once grew on Chesapeake shores and has accepted life in city parks and even in suburban neighborhoods. It is often seen perched alongside a busy highway, oblivious to traffic speeding nearby.

This hawk is, of course, more at home in the swampy woods and flood plains that border the headwaters of so many Chesapeake rivers and streams. Here it places its secure and firmly built nest, usually in the central crotch of a moderately sized tree. A pair may use the same nest for many years, so building it is a long and deliberate process, which may take from four to six weeks.

Rodents constitute the bulk of the diet of this hawk, along with larger mammals, snakes, and amphibians. It occasionally eats small birds, insects, worms, and even fish, but only rarely bothers domestic poultry. It certainly does not deserve the popular name "hen hawk."

This hawk may be recognized by its chunky proportions, the broad bands on its tail, and its rufous underparts. Immature birds are browner and streaked rather than barred on the breast and belly. In flight, red-shoulders of any age show a translucent light patch at the base of the primaries. Frequently, they identify themselves with a piercing, two-syllabled cry.

John W. Taylor

January 22, Long Point, Queen Anne's County

Flying in wide circles over the marshscape, a short-eared owl, hunting, stayed in view for nearly an hour. Passing close several times, it gave me a chance to study its flight. The veering, tilting movement was reminiscent of that of a harrier, but the owl lacked the graceful proportions of the hawk. The owl is less streamlined, its head blunter and its tail shorter.

February 22, Warehouse Creek, Queen Anne's County (by canoe)

Rising from a marshy islet at the mouth of the creek, a short-eared owl flew erratically over the water, disappearing beyond a distant point of marsh. On the tiny island from which it flushed grew a lush stand of phragmites, with some needlerush and big cordgrass—not the usual habitat for the owl, which prefers low, open, meadowlike marsh.

After canoeing across to the point, I flushed the owl again, its flight this time not so erratic. It came to rest, more typically, in a growth of short salt-meadow grass. I enjoyed a closer look, though only a brief one, noting its whitish facial pattern and the strong cinnamon color on the wing. It soon took flight again, displaying prominent black "wrist" patches on each wing.

April 12, Horsehead Farm, Queen Anne's County

Quite early in the afternoon, a short-eared owl took flight from a salt meadow, swinging out over the waters of Prospect Bay. It attracted a herring gull, which made several passes at it. As the owl flew near, it turned its head directly at me, its bright yellow eyes glaring. A pair of red-winged blackbirds also rose to pursue when it came too close to their territory.

Unlike most owls, the short-eared owl is not strictly nocturnal. Still, it is surprising to find one abroad so early. Possibly I had disturbed it in its roosting place.

April 15, Kent Narrows, Queen Anne's County

I hardly looked twice at the gull-like bird flapping leisurely high above the Chester River. But when I did look a second time, the gull became a short-eared owl. The rather long wings were light colored, showing well the dark patches near the bend of the wing. It moved at a steady pace to the north, not with the usual irregular flapping pattern, but with a more direct motion.

At that altitude it was obviously migrating, its eventual destination possibly the tundra on an Arctic shore, or some remote island in Hudson Bay. I watched it cross the water near Eastern Neck Island, in the general direction of Baltimore, until it became a tiny speck in the blue.

The short-eared owl (*Asio flammeus*) is of medium size with small, inconspicuous ear tufts and pale, tawny general coloration. The facial disc is white, bordered with black, and the eyes are yellow.

Unlike most other owls, it is a bird of open country, with a special affinity for marshes. Along the Chesapeake it shows a preference for extensive salt marshes, but will extend its excursions to drier upland fields, particularly where mice are plentiful.

Usually it is seen coursing over hunting grounds in wavering, erratic flight, sometimes skimming low, then rising for a better view. Or it may hunt from a prominent perch, from which it dashes on silent wings after prey. Although often active at night and even in broad daylight, the short-eared prefers to hunt at dawn and dusk.

This owl is basically a winter resident of the Chesapeake, to be looked for from November through April. Although there are early records of this species breeding in the Delmarva Peninsula, the primary nesting ground lies far to the north, on the Arctic tundra. Often, breeding is determined by the available food supply; owls linger to nest where mice and voles are plentiful. Conversely, when food becomes scarce, owls move elsewhere.

John W. Taylor

March 24, Pennington Pond

Heavy layers of ground fog, blown in with a south wind, veil the sunrise, but its light filters through, tinting the haze with opalescent pink and orange. Drifting wisps hide the pond's far shore. Through the mist, like a ghostly apparition, stands the first great egret of the spring, preening on a tuft of broken spartina.

The lores are the bright turquoise seen only during breeding season. The long aigrettes drape gracefully down the back, their tips stained with muddy water. After nibbling briefly at these plumes, the egret begins walking along the shore, feeding.

Fallen grasses, rocked by the easy wave motion, combine with various reflections to create a complex of rhythmic, serpentine patterns both in front and in back of the bird.

June 22, Currioman Bay, Westmoreland County, Virginia (by canoe)

The south end of the large island in Currioman Bay is thickly overgrown with marsh elder and red cedar, mixed with some bare-branched, dying hackberries. Balancing on the topmost branches of this growth are two dozen great egrets and four little blue herons, watching me approach by boat. A great blue heron flaps ponderously toward the mainland.

All three species are breeding on the island. Their nests are quite low and can be easily reached, but most are protected by the thick mass of shrubbery.

Two egret nests on the periphery hold fuzzy white chicks. The chicks are still clad in natal down, which grows longest and thickest about the head, and their bare pink skin is exposed in places. The greenish yellow mandibles are held open, as if the chicks were panting from the heat.

An adjacent nest shelters a great blue nestling, larger than the egrets, and with a proportionately longer and heavier bill. Its pale yellow eye glares at me, more with disdain than fear. The hubbub created by my visit subsides as I paddle away.

July 29, Four Mile Run, Alexandria, Virginia

Great egrets employ unusual tactics to catch fish in these cattail-bordered ponds off the Potomac. Ten egrets float back and forth in easy buoyant flight over the water, stabbing at fish from the air. Maneuvering with the grace and agility, if not the speed, of swallows, they hover over the fish before spearing them with snakelike strikes of their long, sinuous necks and sharp bills.

An unusually high tide covers the flats where the egrets usually fish, possibly accounting for this unorthodox manner of feeding. Or perhaps a concentration of fish is trapped in water too deep for wading.

The great egret (Casmerodius albus) is a species of nearly cosmopolitan distribution, occurring in various racial forms in all but the Arctic regions of the world. The Chesapeake bird belongs to the tropical American race, which ranges from South America to southern Canada.

Most great egrets that breed on the Atlantic seaboard migrate south in the winter, though a few stay through the year, especially if the weather is mild. The earliest migrants return in April, when they may be seen on most Bay tributaries. Some then move father north, while others disperse to local breeding sites.

Great egrets nest primarily on the coast in our latitudes, forming colonies with other herons on isolated barrier islands. Similarly, they join other heronries that utilize the marshy islands in the lower Bay. Smaller numbers of them nest inland in wooded swamps, usually in the company of great blue herons.

After the young have fledged, they join the adults in a general exodus that takes them inland and to the north. It is during this postbreeding period, in August and September, that the great egret is most common and widespread on the Bay.

John W. Taylor

April 12, Pennington Pond

Each day for the past week both snowy egrets and the larger great egrets have gathered along the pond's marshy edges. At times, as many as a dozen are present at once, pausing on their northward migration up the Bay.

The great egrets seem tolerant of one another, but the snowy egrets are highly territorial, chasing away others of their kind that come too close. When a snowy egret becomes angry or excited, it raises its crest, elevates its plumes, and nervously lifts its wings.

Late today three great egrets and one snowy egret perch in trees by the pond. For more than an hour they rest, motionless, except for occasional preening. The afternoon sun accentuates the long, lacy aigrettes that adorn egrets at this season.

August 12, Pennington Pond

A snowy egret on the far side of the pond seemed under stress of some sort. It stood among downed branches on the bank-side, the water lapping at its breast. The bird had assumed an unnatural position and was in deeper water than one would expect. A closer look revealed that it was indeed in trouble, having somehow entangled itself in the vegetation.

I could not reach the struggling egret on foot because of the soft, oozy shoreline. Taking the canoe over, I eventually managed to free the exhausted bird. Its feet were entwined with long, filamentous algae, which had draped the submerged branches.

The egret had become quite weak and, when set free, barely managed to grasp onto a branch of a nearby willow. It made no attempt to fly. An hour later, it was still there, but seemed to be recovering. (The next morning it was gone.)

September 30, Romancoke, Queen Anne's County

Late in the afternoon, two snowy egrets balanced delicately on the tupelos overhanging the water. The leaves of these trees had already turned a rich wine red, which accented the white of the birds. The gracefully curved shapes of the egrets completed the harmony.

Both birds carefully scanned the shallows beneath, looking for fish. In its eagerness, the lower one submerged the branch with its weight. Its feet were in the water.

These feet were brighter yellow than those of its companion, and its bill was darker. The paler feet and lighter bill were the marks of an immature bird. Also, there was less yellow around the youngster's eyes. Such minor differences were noticeable only because the egrets were together.

Soon the egrets stopped feeding, assumed relaxed positions, and groomed themselves, running their bills through breast feathers. The older bird shook itself, ruffling its contour feathers, then lowered them back into place.

They paid little attention to another snowy egret that arrived, circling wide before settling in with the others. The newcomer also began preening, moving its bill through the primaries. It was another young bird, with pale feet and bill.

Perhaps this was a family group, still together months after the nesting season. The three showed none of the territorial hostility that egrets display in the spring. They rested amicably in the warmth of the September afternoon, untroubled by seasonal urges or rivalries.

The snowy egret (Egretta thula) is the smallest of the two white herons found on the Chesapeake, measuring about two feet in length. Its black bill and crested head help to separate it from the much larger great egret. The yellow feet, often shuffled in the water to stir up prey, are also distinctive.

Warm-weather birds, snowy egrets first appear on Bay waters in late spring. Most of them soon migrate farther north or repair to nesting colonies on the coastal islands. Only a scattered few remain the whole summer.

But after the breeding period, the snowy egrets disperse widely. They are most numerous on the Chesapeake in late summer. By November most of them have moved to winter quarters in Florida and on the Gulf Coast.

Their numbers have recovered from early in this century, when they almost faced extinction. Plume hunters slaughtered them for their aigrettes, long delicate feathers worn during the mating season, which milliners used to adorn women's hats.

John W. Taylor

August 30, Cove Point, Calvert County

The weather remains clear, despite the third consecutive day with strong east winds. The stiff breeze, combined with the high tide, has concentrated shore birds, terns, and gulls on the upper beach, where the vegetation offers them some shelter.

A party of sanderlings seeks protection in the lee of a tangled mass of beach grass. Many are dark-backed youngsters, tundra-born this very summer. Two or three still show the dark forewing of juvenile feathering. They are conspicuous among the nearly white adults.

A few sleep, but most are busy preening, assuming a variety of contorted postures. One busily rubs its head against the side of the breast. The neck of another is twisted 180 degrees so that it can reach its upper back, where the scapular feathers are askew. One works on its underwing.

Yet another lowers a wing, fanning and twisting its tail while it nibbles at its rump. Possibly it is stimulating oil flow from the gland there. Several stand on one leg, asleep, and others have the head tucked in the sleeping position, but keep an eye open, firmly fixed in my direction.

August 31, Felicity Cove, Anne Arundel County

The rising tide has almost covered a crescent of sandy beach at the mouth of Jack's Creek. On it, two Caspian terns, with heavy red bills and shaggy crests, tower above a troop of sanderlings gleaning at water's edge. Heads down, bills probing, the plump little shore birds work the inside of the sandy flat, rather than run with the surf, as they often do.

The sanderlings are briefly caught against the setting sun, which tints the water beneath them, and in that moment they seem suspended in midair, tiny ethereal creatures, pausing on a journey that might take them to the extremes of another hemisphere.

September 15, Sandy Point State Park, Anne Arundel County

On the beach at daybreak, a compact band of sanderlings runs in and out with the surf, tiny legs a-blur. The flock as a unit advances and recedes with the same rhythm as the breakers, a living wave. Frantically, the sanderlings snatch up morsels before the water is upon them.

A few retain some rusty red on the breast, traces of the breeding plumage, but most are in their pearly gray winter dress. Their pure white underparts catch the morning light, holding its rich luminosity, while each bird is attended by its own glowing reflection on the wet sand.

They do not tolerate close approach and run along the beach well ahead of me, trying to catch the tiny morsels exposed by the wave action. One pauses, wings poised as if to fly, then runs still farther.

Finally, tiring of this game, they take flight, skimming over the waves and returning to where I had first seen them. Their light coloring, accented by the white wing bars, flickers as they fly with short, rapid strokes. As they lift off, one or two utter a short, hard "twick."

The sanderling (Calidris alba) *follows the sea and keeps to the ocean beaches, only occasionally visiting the sandy shores that border the Bay and its estuaries. It finds its sustenance where the turmoil of the surf flings up bits of sea life onto the beach.*

And it is found on beaches nearly the world over. Nesting in the Arctic regions of the northern hemisphere, it migrates to the southern limits of South America, Africa, and Australia. Its migrations take it to all the continents and islands between these extremes.

Despite such world-wide wandering, the sanderling may be found on mid-Atlantic shores during every month of the year. Numbers of them spend the winter in these latitudes, and still others, probably nonbreeders, may be found in the summer. They are most common, however, at the height of the migration periods, in May and again in September.

The sexes are similar in color, but there are two distinctive seasonal plumages. Sanderlings in migration are changing plumage and exhibit all stages of transition. Winter birds are pale overall, gray on back, and pure white below. In the summer, or breeding, plumage, the head, mantle, and breast show much rusty red. Juveniles show black and tawny buff on the back and head. In all ages, a prominent white wing stripe shows in flight.

John W. Taylor

May 2, Near Fairmount Wildlife Management Area, Somerset County

The tide is ebbing rapidly, flowing through the marshy guts with the gusto of a mountain stream. Dunlins, as well as yellowlegs, dowitchers, and plovers, feed on the newly exposed shoreline. Urgently, with a rapid up-and-down motion, the dunlins probe as if starving.

The body is held low, the shoulders are hunched, and the head is lowered so that the bill remains submerged in the shallow pools. Twice the dunlins abruptly fly off, in wide arcs over the water, then return to the original location, wheeling about in perfect unison.

Most are not yet in full summer plumage, though a few have almost finished the molt. Some look a bit ragged, with a pied appearance. What beauties are those in fresh plumage: rich rust on the back, wings, and crown, and coal black and pure white underneath!

One bird pauses to bathe, spraying water over its ruffled feathers and running its bill through half-opened wings. Then it carefully grooms its snowy chest feathers.

May 6, Mayo Beach, Anne Arundel County

Heavy rains and high tides have flooded the mowed salt meadows behind the beach. The shallow sheets of water attract shore birds, now at the height of their northward migration. On the heavily developed western shore of the Bay, resting and feeding places for them are scarce.

Nearly sixty of these fragile waifs dropped from the sky at midmorning but were gone by midafternoon. The bulk of the crowd consisted of tiny semipalmated and least sandpipers. Seven dunlins, sporting crisp black bellies and russet backs, stood out among them. These larger waders fed primarily in the shallow standing water; the others scattered over the grassy flats.

September 14, Felicity Cove, Anne Arundel County

There is little water in Jack's Creek today, following the rapid passage of a cold front. Many terns and gulls rest on the mud, but only a few shore birds remain: five killdeers, one semipalmated plover, one least sandpiper, and a lone dunlin. This is an unusual assemblage, for it is rare to find any one of these last three alone, away from others of its species.

October 18, Blackwater National Wildlife Refuge, Dorchester County

Dunlins move about, in tightly bunched flocks, over mud flats glistening in the fading light. One party dashes by, close in, swerving and twisting, showing white wing bars and the pale outer feathers of the tail. Every bird banks and turns as one, even when wheeling about at sharp angles. With each turn, they change color: now all white breasts, now all dark backs.

With the changing pattern, they merge into the tree line, appearing then disappearing. And with such swiftness! The wind through their wings emits a hissing sound as they flash by.

A flock rises higher, flickering dark against the sun, then rains down to earth and begins feeding on the flats. The birds feed widely over the exposed shore, keeping in touch with a single grating call. Suddenly the individual notes blend into a loud purring, and every bird is on the wing again.

Formerly known as the red-backed sandpiper in the United States, this widespread and abundant shore bird is now known by its officially adopted British name, dunlin (Calidris alpina). The Russian name for the bird may be translated as black-bellied sandpiper.

All of these names are descriptive. In full breeding plumage, the birds are red-backed and black-bellied; in winter plumage, they are uniformly grayish brown or dun-colored.

The dunlin is medium sized, bigger than the diminutive group of shore birds known as "peep" and smaller than the yellowlegs. The distinctive bill, about one and a half inches long, has a slight downward curve. This bill is a good field mark during all seasons, but especially so in the winter, when the birds are somber-hued and more likely to be confused with other species. Their rich, strongly contrasted summer plumage is unmistakable.

Many dunlins have already assumed this striking coloration when they appear along the Atlantic Coast in the spring. During April and May, thousands flock to the flats and beaches of the Delmarva Peninsula, especially on the Atlantic side. By June, most of them are on their Arctic nesting grounds.

John W. Taylor

March 25, Mayo Beach, Anne Arundel County

Obviously resenting my intrusion, a killdeer voiced her irritation with loud staccato outcries. Flying in front of me, then directly running into my path, she dared me to take one step farther. Then, to my surprise, she tried the familiar broken-wing ruse. Dramatically, she fluttered helplessly before me, one wing hanging limply, and called piteously. Her bright rump feathers were ruffled and exposed.

This feigning act was unexpected so early in the season. It was too soon, I thought, for her to have eggs or young chicks.

March 27, Mayo Beach

Chilly rain was falling, but I again visited the beach. The killdeer left her nest to scold me, revealing four eggs she had been incubating. Larger than I expected, the pear-shaped, buff-colored eggs were scrawled and blotched with dark brown. They were in a cloverleaf pattern, the small ends together at the center.

She bravely guarded her treasure. Directly facing me, she scolded loudly, dropping her wing and spreading her tail when I approached too closely. Her fearlessness permitted careful study of her plumage, exquisite at such close range. Mostly she was soft browns, her tail and rump a rich cinnamon orange. A bright red eye ring accentuated the fiery sparkle in her eye.

April 13, Mayo Beach

The killdeer was still incubating her four eggs. She called nervously as I approached, then walked away rather than confront me or put on a feigning act. The eggs were a telling example of nature's camouflage. Their buff ground color combined with the dark markings to blend magically with the sandy beach margin. Though I have watched the nest for three weeks now, it still requires a bit of searching to find it.

The male flew back and forth over the beach, complaining. He finally came to earth and crouched low in the grasses, as if hiding. Or was he pretending to incubate? Was this another diversion, an attempt to deceive me into thinking the nest was elsewhere?

April 23, Mayo Beach

The adult killdeers showed their usual concern, but now it was for their two chicks. Dainty balls of fluff, the young were already patterned like their parents, only much lighter in color and with a single breast band. They followed closely behind their mother as she foraged in short grass. She did not attempt to feed them, but within a few moments she paused, lowered herself to a squatting position, and fluffed out her breast feathers. The chicks crawled under her, poking out only their heads.

May 8, Mayo Beach

Killdeers are nesting a second time this season. The female is sitting in another depression only a few yards from the previous nest. I stay at some distance in order not to bother her.

One of the young from the previous brood feeds nearby. Though it is only just beyond the downy stage, it bobs and nods just like its parents. The tail feathers have developed long shafts, but are still bare.

The shrill, strident cry of the killdeer (Charadrius vociferus) has earned it both its common and its scientific name. Its voice, which may be heard day and night, is familiar to most country folks, for the killdeer, unlike most shore birds, is at home on dry farmland as well as on beaches and sand flats.

Nesting all the way from southern Canada to Chile, and from coast to coast, the killdeer has a breeding range matched by few birds. In the Chesapeake region, killdeers may be considered permanent residents, for many of them stay the year round. Most move farther south for the colder months, but there is no regular migratory pattern; the killdeer's movements depend on the severity of the weather.

The double breast bands of the killdeer are distinctive. No other wader within its range has two bands. These markings accentuate the pure white chest. The upper parts are earth brown, the rump and tail shading into a bright rufous, which is displayed when the bird feigns injury to distract predators from the eggs or young.

The nest, often nothing more than a shallow depression, is placed in the open, wherever there is cleared land. Farmland, airports, and even golf courses will do if there is gravel available in which to nest. The young are born feathered and are able to run about at birth.

John W. Taylor

May 5, Grandview State Park, Hampton, Virginia

Three whimbrels stand alert in the short cordgrass marsh in back of the beach. They eye me nervously, their tawny sculpturesque heads reaching above the grasses. Wary, mistrustful, they are soon up and away, protesting with a sharply whistled "whip-ip-pip-pip," suggestive of the call of the yellowlegs.

Later, the three are on the open beach, feeding like sanderlings, running in and out with the breakers. They capture small snail-like organisms, possibly periwinkles. Before swallowing them whole, the whimbrels fumble with the mollusks, grasping them clumsily and frequently dropping, then retrieving, them.

May 8, Monie Bay, Somerset County

A high tide floods the marshes by midday, forcing the waders up from the beaches. Companies of dowitchers and dunlins, coming in from the shoreline, disappear after dropping into the tall grass. Many of them nap, securely hidden in thick spartina.

Five whimbrels remain in full view, huddled together on a platform of dried grasses. Two of them doze, their long curved bills tucked into their scapulars.

Later in the day, as the tidal flats open, the whimbrels move out to the open beach, where a dozen others that I had not noticed join them.

May 11, Rumbley Point, Irish Grove Sanctuary, Somerset County

Late in the day, as the sun settled behind tiered clouds of blue-gray, a ragged cluster of birds appeared dark against the light, crossing Pocomoke Sound. Flying about thirty feet above the water, they looked too large to be shore birds, though they showed the same manner of flight. Large-bodied and rangy, they displayed pointed, falconlike wings.

When they passed closer, their long curved bills stood in sharp relief. Then the wild, rippling cry of the whimbrel wafted across the salt meadows. About forty birds, moving in a shifting wedge, fell into a single line when several dropped behind.

Again, then once more, their cries carried faintly from the darkening skies. Gradually ascending all the while, they attained considerable height as they disappeared to the northwest.

I felt especially privileged to have witnessed this, the start of a night's journey that will take them to the Great Lakes by morning, and possibly farther before they rest. Only a few observers have ever recorded whimbrels while en route through the interior to their breeding grounds on the tundra.

Strong of wing and voice, with a long, curved bill, the whimbrel (Numenius phaeopus) is one of the largest, most impressive shore birds. Breeding in northern Canada and wintering in the tropics, it visits the Atlantic Coast only in migration. The spring movement reaches its peak along mid-Atlantic shores in early May; the fall migration spans a wider period, from July through September.

The eastern population of whimbrels (others use the Pacific route) moves up the coast, on its spring migration, as far as Maryland and Virginia. After pausing a few days to rest, the whimbrels undertake the long journey to their nesting grounds on Hudson Bay, via the Great Lakes. It is believed that whimbrels make the trip nonstop; there are few records of them along the way, and these have been only of birds in flight.

It is at the beginning of this awe-inspiring flight to Canada that whimbrels may be seen along the Chesapeake. Flocks of varying size, from a dozen to five hundred, pass over on a northwesterly course, often just as daylight is failing. Observations made near Washington, D.C., are evidence that whimbrels also use the Potomac Valley as a flyway.

This species uses an entirely different route on the return trip in the fall. From Hudson Bay, whimbrels come first to the east, some reaching the coast of Labrador before turning south through New England; they then move down the Atlantic Coast, or offshore.

John W. Taylor

May 1, Near Wenona, Somerset County

Both Forster's and common terns are much in evidence, whirling in a confused mass over the sandy island at the peninsula's tip. Common terns, dark-winged with blood-red bills, perform courtship rituals, presenting and exchanging fish with prospective mates. Forster's terns, lighter of wing and with orange bills, outnumber them.

The noisy melee affords me the chance to study the calls of the two species, which sound much the same. The strident cry of the common tern has a drawl at its end. The Forster's is more nasal and not so drawn out. The Forster's seems to have a wider vocabulary, but perhaps this only appears so because there are more of them. They also have low, rasping calls and high shrill screams.

June 14, Metomkin Island, Accomack County, Virginia

Visiting this barrier island for the first time since last spring, I discover that the April hurricane had changed the conformation of the shoreline. Great quantities of sand have washed up over the salt marsh, and least terns have found the shell-strewn strand much to their liking. A nesting colony, in various stages of the breeding cycle, appears to number over one thousand pairs.

Some terns are feeding downy young, while others have older offspring and still others are incubating. Laid in but a slight depression in the sand, their eggs are the same mottled brown as those of the laughing gull and Forster's tern. The least tern chicks are sand-colored, a grayish ocher finely penciled with dark markings. It is difficult not to step on them.

Near the northern end of this colony, out toward the ocean beach, common terns nest. Their breeding cycle is just beginning. All are still sitting on eggs. Their eggs, also laid in the merest hollow of sand, are a darker mottled brown than those of the Forster's tern. Protesting my intrusion, the common terns hover above, complaining, their wings remarkably luminous against the midday sky.

August 31, Sandy Point State Park, Anne Arundel County

With the incoming tide lapping at their feet, a company of terns and gulls rests on a crescent of sand, extending into the Bay. Their bodies rock and sway with the breeze, yet some sleep, the head tucked into the back. Four terns maintain balance while standing on one foot.

Another tern settles among them, a wriggling fish held crosswise in its bill. Uttering the harsh, grating note of the common tern, it presents the fish to a brown-backed juvenile, which still begs like a young chick. A laughing gull, awaiting its chance, snatches the fish away before the young tern can swallow it.

Nearly cosmopolitan, the common tern (Sterna hirundo) is widely distributed as a breeding bird in Europe and North America; it winters on both coasts of South America, Africa, and Asia. In recent years, it has nested irregularly on the Chesapeake, primarily on islands in the lower Bay. However, it is more likely to be encountered as a transient, during migration or postbreeding wandering.

The nest is usually nothing more than a shallow cavity in the sand, sparsely wreathed with bits of beach grass or sea drift. At times, where grass is plentiful, the common tern builds a more elaborate nest, which reaches six inches high or more. The peak of the nesting season is from June to July.

More frequently seen on the Chesapeake is the Forster's tern, and it takes a trained eye to distinguish it from the common tern. The whitish primaries on the wings of the Forster's are distinctive (they are dark on the common tern), as is the orange bill (red in the common tern). In the winter plumage, a black patch behind the eye of the Forster's does not extend around the nape, as it does on the common tern.

Chesapeake-bred common terns are great travelers. Young birds banded in Maryland have been recovered in Cuba, Haiti, Trinidad, and Venezuela.

John W. Taylor

June 13, Near Quinby, Accomack County, Virginia

The salt marsh is a rippling, prairielike expanse of yellow-green. It looks to be almost entirely of one plant—the smaller form of salt-marsh cordgrass. But the blue of scattered pools and tidal streams relieves the monotony.

The strident and persistent calls of laughing gulls fill the air. Some are in flight, but most stand on marshy tumps or bare mud flats; many sit on nests. Platforms of dead grasses, only a few inches high, the nests are conspicuous, showing brown against bright green. They are formed with a heavier, coarser grass than that growing in the immediate environs, so the gulls must have gathered the material elsewhere.

Most nests shelter two or three eggs, light tan with chocolate blotches. A few nests contain newly hatched young, tawny with dark markings. One egg is hatching, the newborn just beginning to pip its way out.

Highly agitated by my presence, the gulls course the sky and scream incessantly. But as soon as I retreat to a less threatening distance, they return to their nests and resume incubating, though they remain wary and suspicious, lifting the head and neck alertly.

Laughing gulls chase the occasional herring gull that happens to pass near the colony. Because herring gulls often prey upon the young of other species, this reaction is not unexpected.

October 8, Fairmount Wildlife Management Area, Somerset County

The bustling activity of forty or fifty gulls attracts my attention to a shallow pool at the salt marsh's edge. More gulls flock to join this busy assemblage, tightly concentrated on a slim sheet of water. For some reason they have selected this one location, not unlike many others in the broad marshes here, as a bathing arena.

Nearly all of them are laughing gulls; only a few are large, whiter herring gulls. They seem excited, almost jubilant, at the prospect of a bath. Perhaps it is the communal aspect of it that makes the occasion seem so joyous.

What a melee of thrashing and splashing! Showers of spray glisten in the sun as they rapidly dip the head, wings flailing the water. The body feathers are fluffed in wild disarray, and the tail feathers twist oddly sideways.

Some birds pause to rub their heads against their flanks; others move off to preen, stretching awkwardly to groom parts that are difficult to reach. Some splash about for ten minutes or more. A sense of joy and exultation pervades the scene.

Then, for no obvious reason, they all take flight, in noisy commotion, leaving many feathers floating on the water and lodged in tufts of grass.

Although it is not present during the colder months, the laughing gull (Larus atricilla) is possibly the best known of the gulls found on the Chesapeake. Abundant and with a confiding nature, it is familiar and easily approachable. And its striking black hood and loud cackling call make it readily recognizable.

Laughing gulls follow the boats of fishermen, feeding on offal thrown overboard, and they frequent docks and marinas, where they await anything edible thrown to them. They attend ferries and excursion boats, hovering near the stern and dipping to the surface with extended legs to snatch at tidbits.

The first laughing gulls of the year appear in early April, though most do not arrive until several weeks later. They are well distributed on Bay waters throughout the summer, though at present they nest only on the coast. These early summer birds on the Bay are most likely immature and nonbreeding individuals. Their numbers are augmented, in July and August, by postbreeding wanderers and by "birds of the year," juveniles hatched early in June.

These youngsters are a dark, sooty grayish brown. They do not assume the fully adult plumage until their third winter, but laughing gulls have a slim, distinctive appearance at all ages and are unlikely to be confused with the other larger, bulkier gulls.

February 26, Selby Bay, Anne Arundel County

The sky is threatening, and a northeast wind drives dark, heavy clouds. Whitecaps roll across the water, even in the sheltered bay. In the shallows near the inlet, over one hundred gulls, both ring-bills and herrings, have collected.

Despite the imminent storm, they all seem relaxed, calmly expectant. Many stand motionless, as gulls do so much of the time. Others bathe, splashing water over themselves with a jerking toss of the shoulder. A few make short, nervous flights of several feet.

The herring gulls are nearly all brown, with mottled first- and second-year plumages, but among the ring-bills there is an even mix of white adults and browner youngsters.

The ring-bills show a grace and dignity lacking in the herrings. An almost dovelike gentleness pervades their manner and bearing.

May 19, Ramsey Bay, Anne Arundel County

A misty sky hides the sun, low to the northwest, but an eerie silvery light floods the shallows at the inlet. Closely bunched, a large flock of gulls crowds the sand bar. Most are ring-bills, nearly one-half of which are in various stages of immature dress. A dozen Bonaparte's gulls linger, far from their eventual summer destination. Four or five pairs of laughing gulls join them, lifting their heads to cackle at one another.

So excited are these laughing gulls that two pairs attempt copulation, though their nearest nesting colony is perhaps 150 miles away, over on the coast. The other gulls, nonbreeders or migrants, stand by idly, as if waiting for the darkness to come or for the tide to change. A few sleep. Around them swarm clouds of tiny midges, rising from the water. A few birds snap at them, hardly lifting a wing in the effort.

In the strange half-light of dusk, thirty new arrivals, flying in from the river, settle among them, a harmony of soft whites and grays.

September 26, Selby Bay

For the past week or so, the local gulls have become flycatchers. Late each afternoon they take to the air, forsaking beaches and piers. Remaining aloft for hours, they soar in lazy, random patterns, interrupted by sudden dips and swerves in pursuit of their quarry.

All three of the gull species now present take part in this ritual. Ring-bills are the most adept at fly-catching, but laughing gulls are skilled and graceful as well. The bulkier herring gulls are quite clumsy.

November 13, Pennington Pond

The past few mornings, just after sunrise, a flurry of gull activity has graced the pond. An assemblage of ring-bills has performed aerial maneuvers, dipping, hovering, circling, and dropping to the surface. Crisp and immaculate in full adult plumage, they are a dazzling white against the dark water.

Just what they are doing is not obvious. Possibly they seek fish trapped by a falling tide, but only a few times does one light on the surface. They do not seem to be insect-snatching, as gulls do at times. Whatever the motivation, the balletic performance is lovely to watch.

Within a few minutes the ring-bills are gone. Some come to rest on the flats near the cove's mouth, others in the waters of the Bay.

For much of the year, the two common gulls of the Chesapeake are the ring-billed (Larus delawarensis) *and the herring* (Larus argentatus). *Both are abundant during the colder months, and many of them also remain through the summer. Most of those present during the nesting season are immature birds, too young for breeding, though a few herring gulls do nest in these latitudes. The primary breeding range of both species lies well to the north.*

It requires four years for the herring gull to attain the fully adult plumage, and three years for the ring-billed gull to do so. The variety of plumages in these intermediate stages can be confusing, but one can separate the birds by pattern and size. The herring gull is large and chunky, with a heavy bill; the smaller ring-bills have more graceful, dovelike proportions.

Identification of the adults is much easier. The legs and feet of the herring are a pale flesh color, whereas those of the ring-bill are yellow. The dark ring encircling the tip of the bill of the ring-bill is also distinctive.

The two species are virtually omnivorous. They are fond not only of fish and other marine life but also of insects, worms, and grubs; they often follow plows, in agricultural areas, to pick up what is unearthed. Both species are scavengers, consuming garbage and floating refuse.

JOHN W. TAYLOR

Marsh Wren

May 27, Near Ferry Landing, Patuxent River, Calvert County

The ebullient song of marsh wrens sounds from every direction. Some of these fluffy mites can be seen, singing while clinging to slender wind-blown reeds. Others, propelled by their fervor, shoot straight up into the air, sputter "music," then drop, extinguished, back into the marsh. Some cavort in pairs, in antics of courtship. One wren enters an old nest, the structure tattered but still intact after a winter of storms.

June 6, Muddy Creek, off Rhode River, Anne Arundel County (by canoe)

Marsh wrens are having a rollicking time amid tall cordgrasses. Several rise into the air in weak, fluttering maneuvers followed by an odd hovering motion. These flights are obviously related to the courtship performance, though the wrens do not sing while flying, as they often do. But song is everywhere. Three wrens sing in unison, a gushing cascade of sound. Wings aquiver, their bodies tremble with the effort.

The song begins softly, so quietly that it is hardly audible from any distance, rises in crescendo, then trails off at the end.

One wren, busy nest-building, trails strands of cattail leaves, but she is careful not to go to the nest when I am so close.

July 10, Muddy Creek, off Rhode River (by canoe)

A nighttime canoe trip yields unexpected pleasures. Among these is the frequent singing of marsh wrens, long after dark. Several times the wrens break into song as though it were broad daylight. They do not sound as if they are moving about much, and it is too dark to see if they are singing while in flight, as they do in daylight. Joyous, effervescent, and carefree is the marsh wren's song, heard in daylight. At night, however, an aura of mystery surrounds the voices issuing from the tall grasses.

The marsh wren (Cistothorus palustris) can be identified by its habitat alone: any wren seen in tall marshy vegetation is almost certainly this species. (Its close relative, the sedge wren, is a bird of low, wet meadows.) The marsh wren has a prominent stripe over the eye and contrasting light and dark streaking on the back.

The nest of this wren is a large, complex structure, carefully woven with the leaves and stems of marsh plants. About the size of a hornet's nest, the structure has a small entrance hole at one side. Soft material, often the fluffy inflorescence from last year's cattails, lines the cavity. Frequently, the marsh wren builds more than one nest, using one for breeding and others for sleeping quarters and as decoys to deceive predators.

Along the Chesapeake, this species occurs in greatest numbers in stands of needlerush that grow extensively in the salt marshes of the lower Delmarva Peninsula. It is also abundant in areas of spartina, especially where there is a mixture of shrubbery. In brackish tidal marshes, this wren is commonly found in cattail communities, as well as in growths of phragmites. Transients may occur in any tidal marsh and are rarely found in interior marshes.

Some marsh wrens remain in the Bay area the year round, but most move south for the colder months. By mid April, they return.

April 18, Muddy Creek, off Rhode River, Anne Arundel County

The new greens of spring brighten the pale umbers and mustard yellows of the wide brackish marsh. Tints of yellow-green enliven the faded cordgrasses, of which three kinds flourish here. Young spears of cattails reach upward six inches or so, and fresh green leaves unfold on the marsh elders.

Yellowthroats abound here. Several crisply tailored males respond each time I make "pishing" sounds. Their husky, twanging calls issue from every side. One curious bird straddles the tops of two cattail stems, each foot grasping a separate plant.

April 22, Irish Grove Sanctuary, Somerset County

At dawn, an eerie translucence illumines the broad stretch of marsh at Rumbley Point. Wisps of ground fog drift beneath the reddening horizon. Prominent in the chorus of bird song, saluting the new day, are the songs of yellowthroats. There seems to be one yellowthroat every twenty yards, mounted on a cordgrass stem or atop a shrubby marsh elder. They continue singing even when watched at close range.

None sings exactly the same, yet the tone and rhythm are distinctive. There is no mistaking the song: three syllables, repeated three times, "witcheree, witcheree, witcheree."

June 15, Pennington Pond

Yellowthroats are nesting in a marshy cove alongside a stream that enters the pond. The drab little female nervously scolds me while she holds food in her bill, so I believe she has young in the nest. But to find that nest in the wet tangle of briars and vines would be hopeless. She has hidden her treasure well, though she herself boldly appears, her black eyes glistening fearlessly.

She calls nervously, a note with a special timbre or quality all its own. It sounds with more of a twang, huskier and lower pitched, than the notes of other warblers.

July 25, Beverly Beach County Park, Anne Arundel County

A sudden outburst of bird song broke the afternoon quiet. From weedy pond-side growth, a warbler-sized bird mounted into the air and, floating on trembling wings, delivered an ecstatic flow of bubbling notes. A few phrases of the typical song of the yellowthroat identified the singer. The solo ended at the apogee of the flight when the bird silently dropped back into the shrubbery.

This seldom-heard "flight" song of the yellowthroat is usually given late in the season, after nesting is completed. I wondered at the pure joy and exuberance of the performance, which was more intricate and sustained than the normal song given in the spring. What stimulated the virtuoso display by this tiny creature? The breeding season over, there was likely little sexual or territorial provocation.

The common yellowthroat (Geothlypis trichas) is a frequent inhabitant of Chesapeake country for much of the year. Yet few people know it, perhaps because it prefers the dense cover of low shrubbery and briar tangles, usually near water. It finds marshes, both fresh and salt, to its liking, as well as shrubby swamps and even roadside ditches. From this wide variety of habitats, its bright, rapid song can be heard from April through August. It usually consists of a series of three syllables, repeated with considerable variation.

The dark mask around the eye and the bright yellow throat identify the male. Females and immature birds are olive-brown above, with a yellow throat, and they lack the mask.

Members of the warbler family, yellowthroats are insectivorous and repair to warmer climes in the winter, though a hardy few stay year round on the Chesapeake.

John W. Taylor

February 24, Sandy Point State Park, Anne Arundel County

A bare bay-side tree is suddenly foliaged with blackbirds. Red-wings balance on every branch and twig that can support them. Nearly all of them seem, at a distance, to be females. They have just crossed a wide body of water and are quietly resting. I wonder if these are early migrants, pausing on a journey that will take them much farther north, where the males are waiting with staked-out territories.

March 21, Horsehead Farm, Queen Anne's County

A dozen red-wings settle into the topmost branches of a flowering red maple, their bright shoulder patches harmonizing with the reddish masses of blooms. All of them male blackbirds, they soon begin singing very softly, as if to themselves. They seem lost in reverie, possibly induced by the gentle warmth of the spring afternoon. The susurrant chorus continues for fifteen minutes. Interspersed are the usual red-wing calls: a loud "check" and a rusty whistle.

May 20, Pennington Pond

The brackish marsh at the head of the pond measures barely an acre, with narrow fringes extending along the shore. Yet within these limited confines at least four pairs of red-wings nest. In addition, two or three unattached females roam about, so there may be even more nests. It is difficult, without more thorough study, to determine exact relationships, but each of the four males has a well-defined territory. And each has a favored guard post, from which he chases away all intruders. Every male has a singing station, the top of a shrub or a phragmite stem, from which he proudly announces what is his. His enthusiasm often lifts him into the air, where he continues singing. In such close quarters, there is constant confusion, with much posturing and wrangling.

November 4, Elliott Island, Dorchester County

Against a crimson sunset, a swirling mob of blackbirds milled about over a dense growth of phragmites. Many of them settled into the tall reeds, seeking roosting places for the night; most whirled about restlessly. From this feathered maelstrom issued a steady babble of whistling and clucking.

Almost everyone who lives near the Bay knows the male red-winged blackbird (Agelaius phoeniceus). There is nothing shy about him. Flaunting his crimson and yellow shoulders, he mounts the most conspicuous of perches and loudly announces his presence. Wings and tail spread, he puts every bit of himself into his song, a creaking, gurgling "oke-a-leeeee."

Not so well known is the female of the species. She is brown and streaky, sparrowlike in appearance, with no red in the wing. She can be recognized by her size, shape, and typical icterine bill.

Red-wings are among the most abundant of North American birds. Their numbers in some winter roosts are inestimable. At dusk they pass overhead in endless streams.

Red-wings prefer marshy lowlands for nesting, but they may be at home in any open, grassy location if there is sufficient vegetation to hold the nest and to furnish cover and food.

John W. Taylor

September 1, Patuxent River at Hills Bridge, Anne Arundel County

This date, the traditional opening of the hunting season for "rail birds," brings to mind earlier days on the Patuxent. On opening day, and during the peak flight in early September, hunters always poled through the marshes. "Pushers," the local guides, shoved flat-bottomed skiffs at high tide through the flooded stands of wild rice.

But this is a sport of bygone times. Though the season is still open, and a few pushers are still licensed, almost no one hunts the sora rail these days. Marshes and stream beds have silted in so heavily that it is difficult to push the skiffs through the vegetation. And all of the old-time pushers have died.

Though it makes for poor sport, some hunters shoot these rails without first flushing them into flight. Rails make an easy but tempting target when surprised in the open among fallen grasses or on exposed mud flats.

September 12, Near Bristol Landing, Patuxent River, Anne Arundel County (by canoe)

As the tide recedes, leaving muddy margins at the edges of the creek, soras begin calling. The lowering water seems to stir these rails to action. From the marshy tangles issues a variety of whistles and squeaks, from which three different calls can be distinguished. The shrill descending "whinny" is the most prominent, but perhaps more frequent is a quail-like, plaintive single note, given with rising inflection. Yet another cry, a sharp clicking chatter, is like that of the Virginia rail.

Two wary soras walk out of the dense marsh, tails flicking nervously, probing among downed rice stalks. One sora comes quite close, showing its yellow bill and greenish legs. The masklike black about the eye and throat is distinct, and the deep tawny brown of the upper body is especially appealing.

Later, back on shore at the landing, I discover a pile of rich brown sora feathers. A hunting party had evidently cleaned and skinned the day's bag on the spot. Each hunter can legally kill up to twenty-five soras per day.

September 16, Near Western Branch, Patuxent River, Prince George's County (by canoe)

A network of creeks and tidal guts runs through the broad wetlands at the confluence of Western Branch and the main river channel. In winter, the marsh growth here lies flattened and open, providing little cover or concealment. Today, however, the grasses still stood tall, over a man's head, permitting one to hide with little effort.

Seeking a quiet, shady place to nap in midafternoon, I slid the canoe into these rank growths, anchoring it on an island of downed cattails. Effectively camouflaged, I studied the life around me.

A least bittern pranced out of the marsh and stalked fish in the muddy shallows, much in the manner of a green-backed heron. It worked along the shore for ten to fifteen yards before merging back into the tall growth.

A young sora, paler than the adult rail and without the black mask, gingerly stepped into the open, then faded like a ghost into the shadows. I had a fleeting glimpse of yet another sora just as a king rail emerged from the undergrowth. It also was gone within seconds.

Among the birds that live in the Chesapeake marshes, none is more elusive or retiring in disposition than the sora rail (Porzana carolina). It is a denizen of tall, dense aquatic growth, and its comings and goings are cloaked in mystery. Although the sora is not uncommon, one must make a special effort to find it.

To know the sora, one must penetrate its haunts, preferably by boat. If surprised, the bird will take to wing, legs dangling awkwardly, then drop weakly out of sight. But if it senses danger in time, it will skulk deeper into the swampy recesses, vanishing like a shadow.

If the observer sits quietly long enough, he or she may be rewarded by seeing the sora step to the water's edge. Flitting its short tail, it shows rich olive-brown on the back, with a black face and throat. Walking deliberately on long, yellow-green legs, it looks about with a nodding motion of the head.

Soras are transients (though there are a few instances of breeding) on the Chesapeake, appearing when wild rice, a favorite food, is ripe in late August and early September. They winter chiefly on the Caribbean islands and in northern South America.

JOHN W. TAYLOR

January 30, Pennington Pond

A kingfisher reminded me today that fish-eating birds face hard times when their feeding grounds are iced in. Often they can find open water only where currents are strong or where tidal action keeps the water from freezing. Some species move to the saltier, unfrozen waters of the open Bay.

The kingfisher showed special adaptation to severe conditions. Along the frozen pond's edges, ice was covered with a thin skim of water, the overflow of the incoming tide. The kingfisher dropped from its perch into this inch or so of water, then briefly fluttered on the surface. It is not clear whether the bird mistakenly took this to be open water, or if it could see a fish beneath the ice. There may even have been tiny fish in the film of surface water.

The kingfisher returned to its lookout and continued to show a strong interest in the frozen pond beneath it.

March 8, Pennington Pond

A male kingfisher resolved his difficulties with a medium-sized white perch that he had caught. The fish looked larger than its captor. Certainly it seemed too large to be swallowed. But it was a real prize, one not to be relinquished.

Its beak full, the bird managed a rattling cry of conquest. After a pause to collect himself on an oak stub, he attempted to knock the fish against it. But this action was ineffective and almost freed the prey. The task of the kingfisher was more difficult because he held the fish crosswise and, of course, could not swallow it in that position. Twice the kingfisher nearly lost his catch during attempts to shift the fish's position.

The kingfisher tried once more to stun the perch and this time succeeded, at least in making it wiggle less. Then gradually, carefully, with deft little tosses, he grasped the weakened fish at the desired angle.

Somehow, the bird's gape managed to accommodate the fish, which created a wide bulge in the throat. The swallowing process took another ten minutes.

May 20, Pennington Pond (by canoe)

Each spring I wonder where the kingfishers nest, for there are no steep earthen banks nearby into which they can burrow. Today, while canoeing in a less frequented part of the pond, I solved the mystery.

A female kingfisher emerged furtively from behind the exposed roots of a bank-side pine. The bank there is only a few feet high, and much of it consists of a tangle of roots. Deep recesses and hollows afford access to the earth behind it.

The shrewd kingfishers have been quite careful not to show themselves near this site. But now that I know where the nest is, their orientation to the site is quite evident.

The hefty belted kingfisher(Ceryle alcyon) is larger than a robin, with a big beak and a ragged crest. Both sexes are white and bluish gray, but the female is distinguished by a chestnut band on her belly. Except during nesting season, the species is by habit quite solitary.

The female lays five to eight eggs in a chamber, situated at the end of a tunnel dug out of a sand or gravel bank. The burrow's entrances are circular and about four inches in diameter.

The kingfisher is a year-round resident of the Bay area, though there is a decided migratory movement. Nesting birds seek more southern climes at winter's onset, and other birds that breed to the north take their places. These wintering birds are concentrated in the Bay's lower reaches, where they are more likely to find permanent open water.

The kingfisher does not allow close approach but makes no effort to conceal itself. It fishes from an exposed branch over the water or momentarily hovers in the air before diving. It frequently gives its call, a loud, raucous rattle.

John W. Taylor

March 28, Remington Farms, Kent County

Several dozen tree swallows pirouette over the marshy ponds, their backs glistening in the warm spring sun. They are more vocal and musical than usual, and their calls have a sweet tinkling ring. Some show interest in the bird boxes erected here, clinging to the entrance holes and resting on the roofs. It seems too early in the season for nesting, though, and these birds are probably transient and bound for more northerly climes.

April 2, Rhode River, Anne Arundel County

Hundreds of tree swallows dance over the water. They skim the surface, where they find insect life of some kind, despite the brisk northwest wind and chilly temperature. Suddenly, most of them mount en masse into the sky, so high they appear as a trail of smoke. Are they seeking food or merely celebrating the joy of flight? They return almost immediately to the water, where they dip, swoop, and hover, calling all the while, a faint, lively twittering.

May 11, Tuckahoe State Park, Caroline County

A dozen tree swallows skimmed and skirmished over the lake. They haggled over the available nesting sites. Four of them fluttered and fussed at a hole in a dead willow. One clung to the edge of the cavity, while the others buzzed about like bees, looking for a chance to stake their claim.

At a smaller pond nearby, competition was not so strong. A pair of swallows carried nesting material into the end of a pipe that formed a road gate. Cramped quarters! The pipe's diameter was hardly wide enough to admit the bird.

October 4, Cape Henlopen, Sussex County, Delaware

Several thousand tree swallows mill over the horizon, appearing in the distance as a cloud or mist. They whirl over phragmites and collect on phone wires. Many hover over a growth of wax myrtle, feeding on the berries. More swallows are over the beach, many settling among the dunes, where the sand offers some shelter from the strong winds and provides warmth for their tiny bodies. After they spend a few moments on the sand, their vigor is restored, and they are off again. Other tree swallows immediately replace them.

The tree swallow (Tachycineta bicolor) is most conspicuous in late summer and early fall. This is when these birds assemble in great flocks and begin to drift southward. These concentrations primarily occur on the Atlantic Coast, where the birds swarm in clouds over the dunes and marshes. Fewer numbers migrate along the inland river valleys.

The hardiest of the swallows, they are the last of this clan to begin the fall movement to the south. On chilly days, they may be seen resting on the dunes, seeking the warmth of the sandy earth. They may even rest on highways, enjoying the pavement's heat. They often may huddle closely, sharing the warmth of their own bodies.

These swallows seek natural hollows and cavities for their nesting sites. An abandoned woodpecker digging is ideal, especially if it is near water. Bird boxes are often utilized, if situated in marshland or over water.

The tree swallow is recognizable by its steely blue-green back and its clear white breast and throat. Immature birds have brownish upper parts.

John W. Taylor

Barn Swallow

April 6, Selby Bay, Anne Arundel County

Barn swallows have today returned, all the way from South America, and seem overjoyed at being home again. At daybreak, a pair, perched near an old nest under a boathouse, are atremble with song, an endless jumble of sweet chirping. This twittering has much the quality of their ordinary call notes, but is livelier, full of trills and warbling cadences. Another swallow appears, and the three join in chorus, a paean to the dawn sky, the rebirth of spring, and their return.

April 23, Milltown Landing, Patuxent River, Prince George's County

Newly arrived, barn swallows dash and dart in and out of an old tobacco barn, briefly pausing to rest on rafters or to cling to nests plastered under the eaves.

The nests are probably old ones, used last year, for it is unlikely that they could have completed new nests so early in the season. The site also is protected from the elements, so nests from a previous year are most likely well preserved. I see only one bird carrying nesting material.

I count seventeen nests, most placed against the side of a wall or beam, with no support beneath them. Only a few rest on horizontal surfaces. They are chiefly constructed of light, nearly white mud, fashioned in layers made up of pellets about the size of a nickel. Dried grasses lace and strengthen the layers. That the nests last through winter rigors is a testament to the durability of their construction.

May 12, Deal Island Wildlife Management Area, Somerset County

Several dozen swallows swarm around a derelict fishing shack, nearly hidden in the salt marsh. They are nesting on fallen support beams under the building. Swooping and swirling about the weathered timbers, they chatter excitedly, their pleasant demeanor in no way affected by my intrusion.

Some collect mud found at the edges of drying rain puddles. Several of them busily gather mud and bits of grass from a nearby roadside. I wonder how they manage to cram their beaks so full and continue their constant twitter.

I carefully watch those at the puddle. Do they form the wet earth into pellets, then glue them to the nest? Do they grasp the mud between the mandibles, or does it merely adhere to the outside of the bill? I suspect the latter because the swallows apply the material to the nest with a smearing or wiping motion.

The swallows work steadily, taking little time to rest or feed. Several lounge on a rusting pipe extending from the shed, but even these are busy conversing softly among themselves.

The first barn swallow (Hirundo rustica) of the spring is an especially welcome sight. The gentle, confiding disposition and unusual grace and beauty of the barn swallow make it a favorite of many.

Journeying from their winter home in South America, barn swallows arrive on Chesapeake shores early in April. Immediately upon arrival, they inspect previous nesting sites, perching nearby and chattering softly.

They raise their families at our very doorsteps, nesting on porches, under boathouses, and under docks, as well as in barns and abandoned buildings. Their mud nests are fortified with grasses, roots, and other vegetation. When their young have hatched, parents work in harmony, feeding and caring for them for about two weeks. After the young leave the nest, they often return to it each night for four or five days.

As soon as the young are strong on the wing, swallows collect in large flocks, preparatory to the long flight south. Most have left the Bay area by September, though stragglers remain until October.

John W. Taylor

January 31, Ivy Neck Peninsula, Anne Arundel County

Just before dark, a strange hissing scream issued from the woods along Cheston Creek. I suspected that a mammal, possibly a raccoon, was the noisemaker, but as I drew closer an owl took flight and sailed across the water on silent, rounded wings.

When it settled at some distance, it showed the size and shape of a barred owl. Later, as I returned along the same path, I heard a single "whooo-aw" in familiar barred-owl accents.

Audubon referred to a "hissing noise" made by this species that could be heard "on a calm night fifty or one hundred yards," and other writers have mentioned barking calls, much like the baying of a hound. Great horned owls give a similar call.

April 26, Pocomoke Swamp, Worcester County

Falling bark drew my attention to a barred owl, flying across a deep ravine. It came to rest in full view, at medium range, halfway up the opposite slope. Surprisingly tame, it allowed close study as it perched upright, swiveling its head to look back at me. It then flew to a partly dead hackberry tree, the top of which was broken off.

The fallen limb had left a cavity, and peering out of its darkness was an owlet's fuzzy white head. Nearby, grasping a slanting branch, were two more owlets, both well feathered, though one was older and more developed. The latter showed considerable spotting on the head and wings, and a facial pattern quite like that of an adult. The younger-looking owl still showed much down on its breast and head, while the nestling in the cavity was smaller, with fluffy down covering much of its body.

Obviously, hatching had occurred at staggered intervals, incubation having begun with the first egg laid. This instinctive trait apparently protects the young from predation and helps balance brood size with food supply.

June 8, Tuckahoe Creek, Caroline County (by canoe)

For much of the afternoon, the sky was an opaque blue-gray, its light veiled by a dank, heavy atmosphere that hung like gauze over the marshy vistas. Toward dusk the sun emerged, a great orb glowing on the horizon. But heat and humidity persisted, stifling all bird song, except for the dreamy drawl of a wood pewee.

Breaking the hush, three barred owls exploded into a burst of frenzied hooting. The usual "whooo-aws" mingled with grunts, "sneezes," dovelike cooing, and chickenlike cackling. Two owls seemed to have been calling antiphonally, while another accompanied with low barking sounds.

These unearthly sounds, so loud and unexpected, ceased within minutes, though the birds continued to converse in normal tones at intervals.

The barred owl (Strix varia) haunts the bottom-land swamps that fringe so many Chesapeake tributaries. Its center of abundance is in the heavy timber that grows along slow-moving tidal streams such as the Pocomoke, the Patuxent, and the Choptank. It may, of course, be found elsewhere, and on higher ground, but swamplands are the place to look for it.

And to listen for it. Its characteristic eight-part hoot is often the first indication of its presence. It also makes various barking and whooping sounds, especially during the courtship period. The barred owl is more vocal at dusk and in the early evening, but a single "whooo-aw" may often be heard during daylight.

Barred owls are poor nest-builders and in many instances appropriate nests built by other species. Old stick nests of the red-shouldered hawk or crow are frequent choices. Natural hollows and cavities may also be used as nesting sites.

Chesapeake barred owls are sedentary, living year round in home territory, unless displaced by other owls or by habitat destruction. In winter migrants from farther north may join them. A barred owl banded in Ohio in May was recovered in Maryland the following October.

John W. Taylor

September 19, Blackwater National Wildlife Refuge, Dorchester County

A swarm of shore birds, together with a score of terns, suddenly took flight, alerting me to the peregrine that dashed into their midst. Unsuccessful in its quest, it circled over the marshes, alternately soaring and flapping, in the manner of an accipiter.

Moments later it dived at a Forster's tern, which escaped without much effort. Three times the falcon attacked the tern, once falling like a rocket from straight above. Each time the tern evaded the attack.

A dark, heavily streaked immature bird, born this year, the falcon seemed an inexperienced hunter. Or perhaps its attempts were half-hearted, only in play. A mature falcon would have easily captured the tern.

October 6, Eastern Neck Island, Kent County

Late in the afternoon, a peregrine flashed over the small bridge leading to the island, dropped low along the shoreline, then crossed to the marshy point extending into the Bay. It then mounted into the sky and soared in lazy circles.

It was close enough that I could see its dark moustache and even its barred tail when it turned in the light. It soared, much like a raven, for a few minutes, then dropped low over the flats, rousing a group of gulls and scattering a platoon of shore birds.

The falcon briefly disappeared beyond a tall stand of phragmites, then returned and began its fascinating soaring pattern one more. It swooped low again and was lost to sight for about ten minutes.

It came back into view, rapidly coursing over a cornfield and carrying prey in its talons. It came to rest at some distance, in the topmost branches of a dead tree. By driving in the car a bit, then hiking across a field, I was able to study the bird in strong light through the scope. So intent was the falcon on dismembering its captive that I could have most likely approached even closer.

Feathers drifted away in puffs as the falcon pulled and tore with an upward jerking motion. It extracted long pieces of red flesh and intestine, and soon both legs of its prey hung limply astride the branch.

The legs were moderately long, like those of a dunlin-sized shore bird. The peregrine ripped off one leg and discarded it with a deliberate gesture, watching it fall to the ground. I could not determine the fate of the other leg, but it seemed, because no carcass remained, that the peregrine completely consumed the shore bird.

The falcon briefly scraped its bill on a nearby branch, then spent several minutes cleaning its feet. It made a series of up-and-down movements with the bill applied to each foot, then lifted one leg, clenching and opening the talons repeatedly.

After hopping to a higher perch, it took off on a sustained flight over the tree line to the southwest.

Although the peregrine falcon (Falco peregrinus) nests in downtown Baltimore and on the Chesapeake Bay Bridge, as well as at other sites on the lower Bay, these occurrences are, to a degree, artificially contrived. They are the result of a restoration program, initiated more than a decade ago with captive reared birds.

Prior to this effort, peregrines had last nested in Maryland a half-century ago, on the Potomac near Harper's Ferry and along the Susquehanna. It is doubtful if they bred closer to the Bay in recent times.

The tundra race of the peregrine, which breeds far to the north, passes along the Atlantic Coast en route to its winter home in the tropics. Migrants habitually keep to the beaches and barrier islands along the ocean, but at times move inland. They must, of course, cross the mouth of the Chesapeake Bay to reach their destination.

Before making this crossing, many pause at Fisherman's Island or Kiptopeke, near Cape Charles. When conditions are ideal, between fifty to seventy-five falcons may be seen there in one day, the fall flight reaching its peak in early October. The movement north in spring is not so concentrated, and far fewer birds are seen.

The peregrine is recognizable by its large size, its falcon-shaped wings, and the dark "sideburns" or stripes on the side of its head.

John W. Taylor

May 2, Fairmount Wildlife Management Area, Somerset County

An assorted assembly of shore birds peacefully and contentedly feeds on the tidal flats, when two yellowlegs drop in to join it. The newcomers stand a head taller than the others, their grayness conspicuous among the tans and browns of the dowitchers and dunlins.

The yellowlegs remain nervous and alert, bobbing and teetering vigorously. My presence, which does not bother the smaller birds, disturbs the yellowlegs. Their piercing calls shatter the afternoon stillness. Almost immediately, they are up and away, taking the whole flock with them. No wonder that an earlier name for the yellowlegs was "telltale" or "tattler."

May 10, Pennington Pond

The wild, explosive yodels of greater yellowlegs signal their arrival in midmorning. Nine settle on the pond's muddy margins, most likely concluding an extended migratory flight, for they seem quite tired.

Four assume sleeping positions at once, standing on one leg and resting the head on the back (one does not close its eyes, though it blinks sleepily). The others begin feather care and maintenance, running their bills through the secondaries and scapulars and nibbling at their breasts.

Later they begin feeding, prancing about the shallows on spindly legs. At least one continues to give the ringing call, which is consistently four-parted, "teu-teu-teu-teu," rather than in the usual triplets.

Two among the flock are the smaller, shorter-billed lesser yellowlegs. All of both species are in the advanced stages of fresh spring plumage, a more contrasting black and white than the gray of fall and winter. Now they show a crisp, mottled effect on the breast, not the pale wash of umber. Every one retains some brownish gray feathers on the wing.

Remaining in one corner of the pond for nearly four hours, they call sporadically the whole time. They shriek to communicate with one another, yet show neither agitation nor hostility. Yellowlegs just cannot keep quiet.

The turning tide swirls about them, and they begin to move around, probing for food. A flurry of loud yelping announces their intention just before they take flight.

November 4, Jug Bay, Patuxent River, Anne Arundel County (by canoe)

It is a warm day for the season, and the temperature is in the sixties. With the south wind came a very high tide, flooding the fallen, withered marsh vegetation. A month ago the stands of wild rice stood tall, a six- or seven-foot wall of grass bordering the creeks and river. Now they are already browned and toppled, giving the marsh the open, flattened look of winter.

Atop a tiny island of fallen rice stems rests a cluster of yellowlegs. All are sleeping except for one, which warily eyes me. Its alarm note awakens the others.

Reluctant to fly, they hop on one foot to a safer distance. There is an elegance in their relaxed postures, a grace not always evident when they are more active.

The greater yellowlegs (Tringa melanoleuca) is a transient visitor to Chesapeake shores, stopping over on its migratory travels. It lingers a bit on the southward journey, which may take it all the way to the tip of South America, and a few may remain through the winter on the lower Delmarva Peninsula. Usually they are present on Bay marshes from August through November, then return in April and May on the northward move to their Canadian nesting grounds.

The species may be recognized in all seasons and in all plumages by its yellow legs. It is a slim, medium-sized (fourteen-inch) wading bird, flecked with black and white on a gray ground. Its white rump is prominent, especially in flight.

The heavier, slightly upturned bill of the greater yellowlegs distinguishes it from its smaller congener, the lesser yellowlegs. When the two are together, the size difference is obvious. Their voices also help identify them: the greater cries loudly, with three or more descending notes; the lesser cries more briefly, with one or two syllables.

John W. Taylor

April 4, Pennington Pond

The past few evenings, I have heard oldsquaws passing overhead on their migratory flights northward. Their calls, sounding much like they do from on the water, now drop from the spring skies. They begin flying at dusk, when there is little light, and continue until eleven o'clock or later.

Each spring since I have lived on the water, I have heard them. At first I thought they were engaged in some sort of courtship chase, because their strange utterances are much like those of courting pairs on the water, and because such pursuit flights are typical of waterfowl at this season.

Now I am convinced that these nighttime movements are part of the northward migration. Although I cannot see them, I can tell they are flying high and moving to the north directly and swiftly.

The loquacious oldsquaws apparently continue calling to one another during the extended nocturnal journey to their breeding grounds.

December 12, Beverly Beach County Park, Anne Arundel County

Always talkative and sociable, the oldsquaws are today even noisier. Their colloquies echo from far out on the Bay, carrying over the calm waters. Possibly the mild, springlike temperatures excite them. The eerie clamor is made more haunting by the mist, which renders them invisible. There is a mysterious, ventriloquial quality to the sound, which seems to drift in from several directions at once.

All attempts to describe the voice of the oldsquaw are inadequate. None of the transliterations given in books comes close to capturing their music's wild flavor. Certainly the traditional "south, southerly" is not descriptive, nor is "chilhoweee," which is given in some books. And the mingled effect when many birds call at once is impossible to render.

Today, from out of the haze, floats a steady murmur, interspersed with querulous, gull-like chatter and gooselike babbling. Some phrases resemble the squeaking of a door; others, a low-pitched moan. The phrases have been likened, fancifully, to whoops of Indians attacking the stockade in a Western.

December 31, South River, Anne Arundel County

It is a day of fog and drizzling rain. The water is dead calm, its grayness merging with that of the sky. From the murky horizon drifts the unearthly gabble of oldsquaws. Through binoculars, I see their forms in the gloom. The nearest swim above their reflections, as if they float in space. The dim light reduces the greyhoundish shapes of the drakes to simple yet elegant silhouettes. Their long tails, raised above them at sharp angles, provide graceful accents.

I am closer than one usually gets to these sea ducks and can distinguish individual vocalizations. I recognize that what I heard before, in distant cacophony, was only the loudest, final note. At short range, I hear a whining, whirring introduction, like the twang of an unwinding spring.

As the day ends, the fog settles in more heavily, reducing visibility to zero. But the voice of the oldsquaw echoes in the darkness.

The oldsquaw (Clangula hyemalis) is a widespread and common winter resident of the Chesapeake. Oldsquaws prefer deep water, usually keeping well offshore and diving at considerable depths to feed. They seldom come ashore, but occasionally rest on rocks and jetties.

Seen up close, drakes are attractive, with gently tapered bodies and long tails, which turn upward when they are on water. These sea ducks have a unique sequence of seasonal plumages, generally white and brown in winter, and dark brown overall in spring and summer. Hens lack the long tail and are basically grayish brown with a whitish head.

Although oldsquaws are noisy and garrulous, few people are familiar with their calls. One must listen carefully because, though their voices carry a long distance, they often echo but faintly over the water. They often call in flight, rendering it difficult to determine the source of the sound.

They nest far to the north, along the Arctic coasts, where the tundra provides suitable habitat. Circumpolar, their breeding range extends as far north as land exists, and as far south as tundra conditions persist. Most oldsquaws leave the Chesapeake between March 15 and April 15; birds here during the summer are likely to be ill or wounded.

John W. Taylor

January 2, Sassafras River, Cecil County

Pearly gray clouds sheathe the radiance of the sun as it drops near the horizon. Yet its light still glistens on the water, a soft rose pink that brings a long, loose raft of waterfowl into vivid relief. Canvasbacks, necks lifted high, float among smaller scaups and ring-necked ducks. Lesser numbers of black ducks and wigeon swim near the fringes of the main congregation.

The wigeon seem quite attentive to a group of canvasbacks, some of which dive spiritedly and bring strands of vegetation to the surface. The canvasbacks feed hastily, almost voraciously, on this growth, which seems to be some sort of pondweed. One reason for this haste soon becomes apparent.

The wigeon are stealing the pondweed from them! The moment a canvasback bobs to the surface with a morsel of food, a wigeon snatches it away. Somehow, the wigeon senses the spot where the canvasback will emerge, possibly seeing beneath the water's surface.

The canvasbacks are surprisingly docile despite such thievery, possibly because they outnumber the wigeon, and eventually can salvage some of their catch.

Surface feeders, wigeon are unable to dive, and they usually feed in shallow water or on shore, so they resort to theft, victimizing the canvasback, one of the strongest, most able of the diving ducks.

March 5, Beverly Beach County Park, Anne Arundel County

While walking the trail overlooking Deep Pond, in the deepening shadows near dusk, I disturbed two mated pairs of wigeon. The first pair flopped clumsily from underneath the bank and flew only about ten yards before settling back into the water. More curious than afraid, these wigeon looked back to see what had caused the racket above them. They only heard my approach and could not see me well in the growing darkness.

While I admired the soft coloration of this pair, two others swam from under the same overhang. Also unsure of the nature of the disturbance, this pair merely swam toward open water rather than take flight.

At this season, these ducks were in transit, pausing on their journey to the prairie states or Canada. Even so, they were quite out of habitat. On the Chesapeake, wigeon are usually birds of open brackish estuaries and rivers, not of wooded ponds.

These four were but a sad remnant of the flocks that once passed through here on spring migration.

March 6, Selby Bay, Anne Arundel County

The day was warm but grew quite chilly by dusk. Ground fog formed wisps over the water. By sunset a layer of haze settled over the marshes on Long Point. From above, filtered through the mists, came the wild mellow call of the wigeon, "whew, whew, whew."

I could barely see the pair (or were there three ducks?), but I heard the whisper of wings and knew that they were in a mating chase. Several times they passed near me, in swift erratic flight, at first low over the water, then higher above the trees. After dark I could still hear the piping whistle of the drake, delivered in threes, accented on the second, higher note.

Until recently, the soft whistle of the American wigeon (Anas americana) was heard regularly in coves and creeks along the Chesapeake. On moonlit nights, especially, wigeon were vocal, calling as they fed over beds of pondweed. Nowadays most of the pondweed is gone, and so are many of the wigeon.

Only 400 wigeon were counted in the annual winter waterfowl Chesapeake survey in 1990, marking a precipitous decline from the 144,000 tabulated in 1955. Unlike some other waterfowl species, wigeon have not been able to find alternate food sources since vegetative growth in Bay waters has disappeared.

Many locals still prefer the traditional name, "baldpate," for this species because of the white forehead and crown of the drake. A patch of glossy green extends through his eye, a color matched by feathers in the speculum. The chest is pale pinkish lavender, and the back and sides are a finely vermiculated pinkish brown. If the bird is flying, the best mark to look for is the white patch on the forepart of the wing.

The hen and immature wigeon are the most misidentified of ducks, even when in the hunter's bag, where they can be closely examined. They are usually called "gray ducks," a name often applied as well to gadwalls and hen pintails.

John W. Taylor

May 18, C & O Canal, near Widewater, Montgomery County

Splashing water draws my attention to a quiet backwater in a ravine between the river and canal. A brood of bathing wood ducklings is the source of the commotion. The fluffy youngsters, whose down is not as yellow as that of young mallards, bathe with the same actions as an adult. They slap the water with stubby little wings and crane their necks to preen their backs and under their wings.

The impatient mother does not wait for them to finish. She leads them farther down the rocky shore, where she climbs on a half-submerged log and begins to dress her feathers. Her brood clambers up after her, balancing clumsily on gangly legs. Again, the hen shows no patience. She toboggans back into the water within minutes, leaving the poor chicks no choice but to follow her.

May 20, Near Priest's Bridge, Patuxent River, Anne Arundel County

In a pond just off the river, a hen leads her brood of downy youngsters through a floating mass of duckweed. Bits of the plant adhere to the hen's breast feathers and bill. The flotilla leaves dark trails through the light green growth.

Among her charges is a darker, more grayish duckling, with a slimmer bill than those of the others. A tiny hooded merganser consorts with the wood ducks, seemingly quite unaware that it is of a different kind. It dabs at the water just like its comrades, though its species has quite another manner of feeding.

In localities where both species breed, each at times deposits eggs in the other's nest, even though a clutch of eggs may already be present. Both nest in cavities, and, when ready to lay, the females use whatever site is available.

September 4, Muddy Creek, off Rhode River, Anne Arundel County

A company of wood ducks was so intently feeding that my approach was unnoticed, and I had the unusual opportunity of watching them while they were relaxed and unafraid. Easing behind some shrubbery, I moved as little as possible.

Swimming in the creek's narrow headwaters were ten ducks, probably a single family, for only two had adult plumage. The exquisite drake showed no signs of drab summer molt, unusual for this early in the season. The hen was also in near-perfect feather, with a dark, iridescent head and a white "teardrop" around her eye.

Up close, the young birds already showed sexual differences. Drakes displayed light patches on the side of the head, in a faint pattern like that of the adults, and hens had an indistinct eye patch. The streaking of the underparts of the drakes seemed darker and heavier than that of the hens.

Spinning around phalarope-fashion, the ducks picked daintily at the water's surface. Swimming and climbing among the tangled vines near shore, they drew quite near, and I could hear them "talking." Among the soft, finchlike murmurings was a much subdued version of the hen's usual alarm call.

The sharp-eyed mother abruptly lifted her head and rapidly swam out to midstream. The others noticed her tension and followed. Soon, however, they calmed and began feeding again, moving back to the shore.

I had hoped to slip quietly away, leaving this idyllic scene undisturbed, but, as I turned to leave, the ducks caught the movement and leapt into the air, shrieking. At times, it seems, human presence alone is enough to break the poise and rhythm of things natural.

Exquisitely marked and strikingly colored, the drake wood duck (Aix sponsa) ranks among the most beautiful of waterfowl. A crest of green and purple flows from the crown, and the sides of the head reflect the same colors, enhanced by a hint of bronzy yellow. The bright red on the bill and the harlequinlike streaks of white on the head and flanks provide strong accents.

The drake's yellowish tan sides are delicately vermiculated with black, and his dark burgundy flanks are decorated with long, ocher-colored plumes. The wing speculum, which can usually be seen even when the bird is at rest, shows vibrant purples and blues. The demure hen, somber in comparison, also shows glints of iridescence in her predominant blues and grays.

Wood ducks breed throughout their range, which extends from Florida and Texas north to Quebec and Ontario, then west to the Dakotas. A disjunct far western population is primarily coastal in distribution.

Along the Chesapeake, the wood duck can be considered a year-round resident because it may be seen during any month. However, most wood ducks have gone south by mid November, and very few remain after the first freeze. They return early in March.

They commonly nest in the bottom-land swamps that fringe many Chesapeake tributaries, and their only requirement is a hollowed branch or trunk, either a natural cavity or an old woodpecker excavation. They do not attempt nest-building and lay their eggs on the floor of the opening. As the eggs are laid, the female plucks down from her own breast to provide warmth and softness.

January 13, Ivy Neck Peninsula, Anne Arundel County

After three days of rain and misty weather, the air has turned clear and crisp, behind a brisk northwest wind. Seeking shelter from the wind, about five hundred canvasbacks congregate in Canning House Bay. Most doze or float about lazily, but several dozen feed close to the shore. The noble heads of the drakes glisten a deep bronze, and the eyes resemble crimson jewels. Several drakes walk in the shallows near shore, feeding like teal, with a sifting, sideways motion of the bill.

Already some feel the mating urge. From over the water come the strange, guttural notes of the courting drakes. But there are no head throws or any of the ardent pursuit and posturing that will take place in coming months.

At sunset the water shines like a great sheet of pinkish tin foil, with glints of light blue.

February 24, Meredith Creek, Anne Arundel County

A mixed gathering of several hundred diving ducks is massed close to the shore, at the mouth of the creek. Equal numbers of ruddy ducks and canvasbacks swim with a smaller contingent of scaups. Nearly all are asleep, heads tucked into back feathers, floating peacefully in the still water.

After a while, several canvasback drakes begin to stir. They swim after the sleeping hens, even gently nudging them. Occasionally, a drake throws back his head with a stiff, almost comic gesture, the crown nearly touching the rump. A throaty croaking, almost a cough, quite low in volume, accompanies these actions. The sound is so muted that it is difficult to trace its source. It seems to float in the air, to pervade the atmosphere like an odor. Drakes make the sound without opening their bills, with only a slight swelling of the throat.

The hens show no response to all this attention. Many remain asleep even when touched by an ardent suitor. One hen is attended by six drakes at once.

November 24, South River Farms, Anne Arundel County

The dawn was gray, and a wet wind blew much of the morning, but it was from the south and the afternoon is warm and sunny. The wind brought an unusually high tide, which flooded the lowlands on the point, leaving water to glisten in newly formed channels. The cottony white of the groundsel bush still frosts the tawny marshes, outlasting even the flowering asters.

A raft of two dozen canvasbacks sleeps in the afternoon sun, the low light catching their white bodies, burnishing them with coppery gold. Five more ducks splash in, sliding with feet splayed and extended. One splendid drake bathes, spraying water like a robin in a backyard puddle. Another stands upright in the water, exercising his wings.

Other canvasbacks, closely bunched, begin feeding. They dive with a strong, arching roll, disappearing with a flourish beneath the water. When they pop back to the surface, there is no sign of what they fed on. Often, when feeding on underwater vegetation, they bring bits of it with them to the surface.

The canvasback (Aythya valisineria) has the short, stocky look of the diving duck. The drake can be recognized, in flight and on the water, by his white back. Up close, his reddish brown head can be seen in distinctive, sloping profile. The female is grayish overall, with but a suggestion of rust on her head and neck.

Historically, perhaps no other bird has been so closely associated with the Chesapeake. Once, it came in uncountable legions each fall to the shallows of the upper Bay, where it fed on beds of wild celery. More than one-half of the entire continental population of canvasbacks wintered on the Bay and its tributaries. The area's best restaurants featured roast canvasbacks. A famous Audubon painting depicts the birds with the Baltimore skyline as a backdrop.

But that was long ago. Within the past two decades, the canvasback has suffered a grievous reduction in numbers. In the early fifties more than 250,000 canvasbacks wintered in the Bay area. The most recent count (1991) totaled only about a tenth of this figure.

The disappearance of its basic food plants from Bay waters, combined with loss of suitable habitat on its breeding range, dealt a severe blow to the species. Those that presently winter in the Bay region subsist largely on small clams and other invertebrates.

List of Plates

Frontispiece.
Great Egrets in Reeds
1989
Opaque watercolor on tinted board
24″ x 15″
Collection of Mr. Thomas Kline

1.
The Loafing Place: Blue-winged Teal
1991
Oil wash on board
14″ x 21″
Collection of Mr. and Mrs. Donald Hull

2.
Mist on the Tuckahoe: Black Ducks
1985
Watercolor on paper
16″ x 24″
Collection of Don and Lee Schatz

3.
On the Alert: Pintails
1991
Watercolor on paper
17″ x 24″
Collection of John and Nikki
Clementson

4.
Misty Pines: Mallards Jumping
1981
Watercolor on paper
22″ x 30″
Collection of Fontaine Disney

5.
Honkers at Eastern Neck
1989
Oil on board
22″ x 30″
Collection of Mr. Ken Riggleman

6.
Tundra Swans in the Snow
1990
Oil on canvas
24″ x 30″
Collection of the artist

7.
Over the Dunes: Snow Geese
1990
Oil on board
22″ x 30″
Collection of Mr. and Mrs. Donald
Munson

8.
Green-winged Teal in a Snowy Marsh
1991
Watercolor on paper
17″ x 24″
Collection of Mr. and Mrs. Donald
Munson

9.
Jug Bay on the Patuxent: Great Blue Heron
1987
Acrylic on board
20″ x 36″
Collection of the Anne Arundel
County Parks and Recreation

10.
Black-crowned Night Herons
1990
Oil wash over pencil
17″ x 12″
Collection of Mr. and Mrs. Donald Hull

11.
In an Autumn Maple: Green-backed Heron
1991
Oil wash on board
17″ x 14″
Collection of Mr. and Mrs. Chris Wagnon

12.
Chester River Vigil: Bald Eagles
1989
Oil on board
30″ x 24″
Collection of Mr. and Mrs. William Brown

13.
Jug Bay Ospreys
1989
Oil on board
24″ x 32″
Collection of Maryland National Capital Park and Planning Commission

14.
Vantage Point: Northern Harrier
1990
Oil wash over pencil
17″ x 14″
Collection of Mr. and Mrs. Donald Hull

15.
Patuxent Overlook: Red-shouldered Hawk
1991
Oil on board
20″ x 16″
Collection of Mr. and Mrs. Dana Green

16.
Day Begins at Dusk: Short-eared Owl
1991
Oil on board
16″ x 12″
Collection of the artist

17.
Daybreak at Blackwater: Great Egrets
1989
Watercolor on paper
10″ x 15″
Collection of Mr. Thomas L. Shaffran

18.
Snowy Egrets in Loblolly Pine
1990
Mixed media on board
25″ x 17″
Collection of Richard and Pat Piluk

19.
Running with the Waves: Sanderlings
1988
Acrylic and watercolor on paper
22″ x 30″
Private collection

20.
On the Beach: Dunlins
1989
Pencil with oil wash
11″ x 14″
Collection of Joe and Kathy Long

21.
Killdeers
1991
Mixed media on board
12″ x 17″
Collection of Glen and Ruth Cassell

22.
Whimbrels at Low Tide
1991
Oil on board
12″ x 16″
Collection of the artist

23.
Late Light on the Dunes: Common Terns
1991
Oil on board
12″ x 16″
Collection of the artist

24.
On the Pilings: Laughing Gulls
1991
Acrylic and oil on board
18″ x 15″
Collection of Mr. and Mrs. Donald Hull

25.
At Tide's Edge: Herring and Ring-billed Gulls
1990
Oil on board
13″ x 19″
Private collection

26.
Marsh Wrens at Home
1990
Oil wash over pencil
17″ x 14″
Collection of Mr. and Mrs. Donald Hull

27.
Marsh Denizens: Common Yellowthroats
1990
Oil wash on board
16″ x 12″
Collection of Chris Swarth and Marilyn Fogel

28.
Red-wing on Cattail
1988
Watercolor on paper
17″ x 14″
Collection of Mr. and Mrs. William
Brown

29.
Sora Rail in Wild Rice
1991
Oil on board
17″ x 12″
Collection of Mr. and Mrs. Brooke
Meanley

30.
In an Autumn Tupelo: Belted Kingfisher
1988
Watercolor and acrylic on paper
24″ x 17″
Collection of Mr. and Mrs. Kenneth
Hurst, Sr.

31.
Resting in the Phragmites: Tree Swallows
1990
Oil on board
12″ x 16″
Collection of Mr. and Mrs. Don Unger

32.
Barn Swallows in Willow
1989
Watercolor on paper
17″ x 14″
Collection of Sean and Diane
McNamara

33.
Barred Owl in Sweet Gum
1988
Oil on board
24″ x 18″
Collection of Joe and Kathy Long

34.
On Passage: Peregrine Falcon
1979
Oil on canvas
30″ x 20″
Collection of the artist

35.
In the Shallows: Greater Yellowlegs
1991
Oil wash on board
14″ x 19″
Collection of Bill and Linda Raivel

36.
A Chase in the Mist: Oldsquaws
1990
Oil on board
12″ x 16″
Collection of Mr. and Mrs. Donald
Munson

37.
Reflections: American Wigeon
1991
Watercolor on paper
17″ x 24″
Collection of Mr. and Mrs. Donald
Munson

38.
October Wood Ducks
1990
Oil on board
18″ x 24″
Collection of Mr. and Mrs. Donald
Munson

39.
Afternoon Light: Canvasbacks
1989
Oil on board
12″ x 16″
Collection of Alan and Gail Van
Winkle

Acknowledgments

My greatest resource in the preparation of this book has been my wife, Marilyn. From the beginning, she provided encouragement and insight, as well as advice and constructive criticism. She cast a fresh and perceptive eye on both the text and the paintings and shared many of the birding experiences that inspired them.

Katherine Maugans and Matthew Perry reviewed the manuscript and offered valuable, helpful suggestions. Others who offered advice and assistance were William H. Brown, Richard Dolesh, Ben Hrenn, Greg Kearns, Bates Littlehales, Jeff Mauck, Brooke Meanley, and Vernon Stotts. Gene Deems was indispensable in matters involving the Maryland Department of Natural Resources.

I am especially grateful to the director, Jack Goellner, and the staff of the Johns Hopkins University Press. It was they who saw the potential for this book and guided, cajoled, and coaxed it into completion. Henry Tom lent his expertise in clarifying and sharpening the focus of the book, and Jane Warth, with the utmost patience, corrected, refined, and strengthened the text. To Ann Walston goes the credit for the pleasing and effective layout and design.

Birds of the Chesapeake Bay

Designed by Ann Walston

Composed by Brushwood Graphics, Inc.

Printed and bound by Toppan Printing Company (America), Inc.